HOPE
FILLED

A Publication by Heartcry for Change.
Heartcry for Change I CMS House I Watlington Road I Oxford I OX4 6BZ
UK Heartcry Trust UK Registered Charity 1076993 (www.heartcryforchange.com)

ISBN: 9798872473336

HOPE FILLED
by Rachel Hickson

Book cover and content layout designed by Ronald Gabrielsen.

Edited by the Heartcry for Change Publishing Team.

First Edition – Published and Printed in January 2024

HOPE FILLED

RACHEL
HICKSON

CONTENTS

HOPE FILLED

Dedication 7

Acknowledgements 9

Endorsements 11

Introduction — A hope filled life 15

Chapter 1: HOPE FILLED — May God fill you with hope 17

Chapter 2: HOPE FILLED — There is hope for the tree 29

Chapter 3: HOPE FILLED — In the face of delay and disappointment 43

Chapter 4: HOPE FILLED — For my health and emotional wellbeing 61

Chapter 5: HOPE FILLED — When hope seems hopeless 79

Chapter 6: HOPE FILLED — For our financial future 95

Chapter 7: HOPE FILLED — For our friends and family 115

Chapter 8: HOPE FILLED — For the nations and our world 135

Chapter 9: HOPE FILLED — With great expectations 149

About the author 155

About Heartcry for Change 157

DEDICATION

I dedicate this book to Anna Farley.
You ran your race with dignity and courage.
You were hope filled to the very end.
We prayed together, dreamed together
and you were an inspiration of hope
to many in our church.

Thank you, Anna, for all you gave us in fun, laughter
and a continuous challenge to look for more!

I dedicate this book to many friends
who have endured hardship and decided to hope anyway.
You are heroes, who live with a God filled perspective,
in the midst of challenge, loss or pain.

Thank you for encouraging me with your wisdom
and experience on my tough days.

I dedicate this book to an army of hope filled warriors
who face the statistics concerning our nations and homes
and see a bigger picture of Jesus.
You are a wave of joy and love that shifts the atmosphere
of hopelessness gripping our nations.
You are the carriers of hope in the wilderness!

If you are one of these people:

THANK YOU!

ACKNOWLEDGEMENTS

This part of the book is always impossible to write!
There are so many people who deserve
my thanks and recognition

THANK YOU - THANK YOU!

Firstly, I do want to thank my husband, Gordon.
You have hoped against hope for my life, especially
after the road accident.

You are always so excited each time I write a book,
and this time you have written an amazing poem
to end this one.

I want to thank Helen Azer, my friend and kindest critic,
who has laboured with me.

She is an incredible hope filled person.
Again and again, she has inspired me to be hopeful,
after a difficult day.

I also want to thank my army of generous friends,
especially Pauline Azer with her sharp eye for a manuscript
and Sarah-Jane and Alistair Biggart who provided a home of
inspiration in Scotland, where I could write.

Thanks to the many others who have read the
manuscript, advised me and given me hope
that this is a book worth reading.

Thank you for all your various partnerships
with this project!

Finally, thank you for buying this book.
I hope that it will be more than just another book,
but that it will help you understand the journey of life we walk
and enable you to hold fast to your hope in challenging times,
and then shine with inspirational HOPE.

So now - please sit down and enjoy,
get prepared for this next journey of hope,
knowing that God will sit down with you,
and lead you into your

HOPE FILLED LIFE.

ENDORSEMENTS

COLLETTE DALLAS

After over forty years of seeing God move in Africa, Asia, USA and Europe, Rachel Hickson has seen first-hand that nothing inoculates a life against hopelessness and despair like the hope in God's unfailing love.

Join my dear friend and mentor as she uses scripture and stories from her own life to teach us how to live life not with blind optimism but radical hope.

Used as a devotional, this book, along with its very practical activations, will provide a much-needed road map to help us navigate today's world. It will empower you to press into God and to "ask the intelligent questions" so that you can live a hope filled life regardless of your circumstances. Recalling lessons learned through her own life, "Mama Rachel" teaches us how to press through the door of hope in times of trouble and smell the scent of hope instead of the stench of hurt, rejection and loss. She teaches us how to live with expectation and faith that declares "I know a God who can!". She teaches us how we can find hope for health, finances, friends, and family, whilst gently reminding us that we are "seeds of hope" called by God to take His hope and share it with the nations and our world.

Rachel is one of my greatest encouragers and I believe that she has written this book to encourage you too. May this book cause you to hope in God and may He, the God of hope, "fill you with all joy and peace as you trust in him, so that you may overflow with hope by the power of the Holy Spirit". Romans 15:13

— **Collette Dallas**
   Prayer and Prophetic Leader,
   Headway Ministries and Prayer Storm

JOHN MCGINLEY

Prepare to be baptised with hope as you immerse yourself in this amazing book. Stories to inspire you, rich insights from God's word, permission to wrestle with questions, and the challenge to carry the seed of hope God has given you into this world. Read this book slowly, pausing to engage with the spiritual exercises Rachel gives you, and God will set you free from wrong thinking, create a fresh thirst for Him and fill you with his hope-giving presence.

— **Revd Canon John McGinley**
   Lead of Myriad Church Planting Initiative

NICOLE CLARKE

I first met Rachel 20 years ago when she was preaching at Aylesbury Vale Church. Rachel laid hands on me and I crumpled like a sack of potatoes under the weight of Holy Spirit so I hang on every word God speaks through her. Our relationship has grown from being a groupie (so very true) to a most incredible friendship. Rachel's hunger for God, prophetic ear and intentional living are incredibly contagious. We have recently journeyed a painful season with the loss of a dear friend and pastor. Rachel's defiant hope in our loving Heavenly Father has helped our church heal and dare to hope again, especially when it's painful and costs us dearly. I cannot wait to dive into this book again, but this time together with a group of women who wholeheartedly believe that Jesus Christ is the hope of the world. I believe that Hope Filled is a prophetic word straight from the throne-room of Heaven. Let the truth of this book be water to your soul and feed the dry and weary bones.

— **Nicole Clarke**
  Sisterhood, Hillsong Oxford

A HOPE FILLED LIFE

I want to be one of those people who inspire, encourage and lift up the faces of those who feel overwhelmed and give them a revelation of God's hope filled life. I love the carefree, exuberant, hope filled lives of children. "Granny, have you got a present for me?", they will shout with eager expectation! I have six grandkids and all of them have a high expectation of fun when Gordon or I walk into a room. They expect to be spoiled, kissed, celebrated and loved. They run into the room, faces held high, asking for treats and love, and we are very happy to fulfil these hopes and dreams for them. As you imagine this scene, you can have a secret smile to yourself, reflecting on the innocence of the audacious expectations of children, so easily expressed all around us. But we can feel we are now wiser and beyond such wild imaginations; we live in the real world! But the Bible challenges us to keep every sense of hope and expectation alive. In Corinthians we read the following verse:

> And now these three remain: faith, hope and love. But the greatest of these is love.
> **— 1 CORINTHIANS 13:13**

Here the Bible instructs us to ensure that faith, HOPE and love are all evident in our lives all the time. To live life well - HOPE must remain! We need this emotion of hope, an ability to dream, carry excitement and expectation and to be able to believe for good days ahead. But living in our culture today, we have become more and more sceptical, and living with a hope filled perspective seems naive or a dangerous risk. We carry this proverb, this repetitive narrative in our minds, "Don't hope too much, you will only get disappointed!". Our experiences of life train us to become cynical, reluctant and cautious instead of carefree and hope filled. We downgrade our hope and expectations and settle for a "realistic" expectation of life.

Most of us have experienced disappointments or delays that have challenged our hopes and dreams. So how do we live an authentic life where our hope can still stand? Can we truly live a hope filled life in a hopeless world?

As you pick up this book, I trust that your hope will be revived afresh! Each chapter will consist of three parts:

a) teaching on an aspect of biblical hope and addressing the major objections and pastoral issues surrounding hope.

b) encouragement to overcome the obstacles discussed and apply the concepts learned, exercising faith and learning to pray through the barriers and believe for breakthrough.

c) real life testimonies from those who have experienced breakthrough in the area of hope discussed in the chapter.

As you read these pages, I trust you will have a revelation of God's hope that can fill you entirely! He promises you a hope filled life. So let the truth of His word in these pages strengthen your soul… and enjoy living a life rejuvenated with fresh hope!

Rachel Hickson, September 2023.

1

HOPE FILLED

May God fill you with hope

> "To eat bread without hope is to starve to death slowly."
> — **PEARL S. BUCK.**

This was hope fulfilled. Clutching a precious set of keys in my hand, I surveyed the scene. The plans I had for each room were swirling in my mind. I felt I could dance, scream and laugh, all at the same time. Months of paperwork, telephone calls and sleepless nights of planning, had finally been rewarded. I had the keys to a house that would now become our family home. God had done a miracle and we had bought this house against all the odds. God had helped us financially and practically. It felt as if life in the UK could finally begin. Mission accomplished, and my heart felt full.

A spark of hope, awakened in your being, can reset the direction of your life. It is that "get up and go" fuel that sets you on a course of decision-making to fulfil your specific dreams. It is a powerful motivator that urges you to grasp your potential and make it a reality. It is a catalyst that shapes your belief systems. Hope stirs us to look into the future, giving us the courage to move from the security of our present place, knowing something greater is ahead. We all know life feels good when we are hope filled. However, when hopelessness controls our thinking, depression and dark moods can quickly settle, like thunderclouds, upon our soul. If we lose hope, something gnaws away at the joy of life in the inner depths of our being and robs us of this vital sense of wellbeing. As this quote by Pearl Buck bluntly states, living life without hope is a stark experience. Aware of the danger of living with no hope, we often turn to different activities to try to awaken fresh hope again: we may try a new routine of life or exercise pattern, trusting this will rejuvenate our dwindling hope. We instinctively know that without hope we do not function well. We need to live a hope filled life. But how?

The wonderful fact is that God has already designed the way for us to live a hope filled life without stress. All we have to learn is how to receive His hope by receiving His power in our lives. This is not a difficult process. Everyone can live a hope filled life. Here in Romans, the apostle Paul shows us the way:

> May the God of hope fill you with all joy and peace as you trust in him, so that you may overflow with hope by the power of the Holy Spirit.
> **— ROMANS 15:13**

Our amazing God can fill us with hope as we trust in Him. This hope is a free gift, available to you now, however confused, stressed or challenged you feel. God has a gift of hope for you – today!

All around us today influencers, websites and advertising promote schemes to help us feel good about ourselves and life. There are so many techniques publicised, each promising to revive our wellbeing of life, and renew our hope filled perspective. Usually, these courses demand that we first need to be still and empty ourselves of all our stress if we are to achieve a new state of peace. Many of the popular books give detailed self-help techniques for the wellbeing of our emotions. We are advised that to find the solution to our hope deficit, we need to practise various thought rituals, dietary disciplines or specialist exercises. Some people say yoga is helpful when trying to reset your emotional reservoirs, but I am not convinced this is the right way at all. Yoga has a philosophy of challenging you to empty yourself of your stress and, once you have found your empty spot, then you can find peace. But the Bible shows us a different way, in fact an opposite way of thinking! The biblical view advises us to come to God thirsty and hungry and let Him fill us. We do not have to empty ourselves first; He will fill us and satisfy our need for hope directly. We can come to God hungry, lonely, exhausted and He will fill us. Let us remind ourselves of this scripture in Romans once again. It promises us that the God of hope will fill us so that we overflow with hope by the power of the Holy Spirit. We do not have to provide the energy or the effort; we just have to position ourselves to receive by the power of the Holy Spirit and God will fill us with hope. What a gift!

ACTIVATION

Take a moment to pause and receive this gift of HOPE.

Just simply pray and take this verse in Romans 15:13, "May the God of hope fill you with all joy and peace as you trust in him, so that you may overflow with hope by the power of the Holy Spirit." and ask God to fill you.

Remember, this God of hope is ready to fill you. Identify those areas where you feel hope is depleted; name them and ask God to fill you by the power of His Holy Spirit.

A HOPELESS CASE

Not again! The humiliation. The thought of attending yet another meeting, limping awkwardly while everyone watched and then offered to pray for me and nothing happened, exhausted me.

I had been involved in a serious road traffic accident in 1984 which had severely fractured both of my legs. I had been in a coma for five days because of multi fat embolisms that had coursed through my bloodstream, finally settling in my brain stem. There was little expectation that I would survive this ordeal as I lay in the hospital in Harare, Zimbabwe. But I did. Five days later, and after the faithful prayer of many people, I woke up from the coma alive. But although my brain had experienced a miraculous healing, my fractured legs were still broken. Four years later I was still wrestling with the continued pain and limitation of legs that did not work adequately. Gordon and I were now living in the Philippines, working with Reinhard Bonnke. We were seeing miracles transform people's lives every day but my own stubborn legs seemed to be resistant to all prayer. I had seen some slow, gradual movement return but walking was still a struggle, especially without help on stairs. So here I was in the Philippines, being invited to special healing meetings hosted by Charles and Francis Hunter. I felt nervous. I did not have the stamina to face another disappointment. I had carried a word in my spirit since October 1984, just after the accident, that I would be healed. I was considerably better now so maybe I should just be grateful for my life and the mobility I did have and leave it at that. But this promise from Hebrews just gnawed at my being – "For the lame shall no longer be disabled but rather healed". Gordon asked me once again, "Are you coming to the meeting with me?" I was trying to summon the resolve to go to this service and cope with another prayer time and the possibility of more disappointment. My hope was gone.

Eventually I decided to go and found a place at a table away from the main stage. The meal was delicious and people were kind and friendly and, eventually, I began to relax. Then Charles Hunter stood up to speak. Before he had even opened his Bible, he strolled over to where I was sitting, and suddenly, to my horror, I realised he was coming to me. He stopped right in front of me and asked me a question. "Excuse me," he said, "have you been involved in a car accident?" "Yes", I replied. "Do you have any injuries resulting from that accident that still trouble you today?", he then asked. "Yes", I replied again. Immediately many emotions were tumbling inside me: one part of me was excited and my hope was stirring – could this be my moment? Another part of me was frozen rigid – what if nothing happened? How would I cope with another failed prayer time and the repeated disappointment? Before I had even addressed my inner turmoil, I realised that this man was praying for my legs. His prayer was softly spoken and very ordinary. It was short and simple. "God, please heal the damage and trauma caused by this road traffic accident and return these legs to their original design. Thank you!", he prayed. Suddenly he turned his attention to me and asked me to walk towards him and do something I could not do with my legs before he had prayed. I felt no change in my legs; there was no sensation of heat or anything in my legs. I felt hesitant to move. Again he asked me to stand and make a move. Reluctantly I stood up and decided the best test was to remove my shoes and see if I could walk without them or, better still, put both my heels down on the ground. As I took my shoes off and began to force my heels to the floor, I suddenly realised they were straight and weight bearing evenly, with both feet completely connecting with the floor. As my heels hit the carpet, my tears began to flow.

Ever since the accident I had not been able to walk anywhere easily without wearing shoes because my right leg was twisted and much shorter than my left. I simply could not get my right heel to touch the ground. Apprehensively I had taken my left shoe off first and then my right and had now found that, for the first time since the accident, both my heels touched the ground. I knew at that moment that God had miraculously lengthened and straightened my right leg. The pain subsided and I have been able to walk perfectly ever since that time. When I least expected it, God had answered my cry. When I had had no hope, he had healed me. I was literally a hopeless case – but God healed my legs. Suddenly I knew the kindness of God and I was hope filled again. The season of barrenness had ended. I had my legs back…but, better still, I had my hope restored too! This will be explored further in Chapter Four.

EXPECTANT OR DISAPPOINTED?

Your instinctive response to a suggested new adventure often reveals the true state of your hope capacity. If you find yourself immediately sighing with a sense of "here we go again!", accompanied by an instant negative reaction, your ability to hope has probably been damaged. Sometimes we do not even realise that we have downsized our expectations due to repeated disappointments. We still believe that we are ready for a new adventure and that we are truly prepared to navigate the risks involved. However, when the plans become more concrete, we suddenly find ourselves backtracking and wanting to remove ourselves from any risk entirely. We are not sure we can trust so, although we long for the adventure, we are afraid to hope that this time the outcome will be any different. After repeated delays, our hope tank needs healing to help us to trust again.

We read the story of Zechariah and Elizabeth in Luke chapter one in the Bible. They had both lived with repeated disappointment for many years. They both wanted a baby and, even though they served God and lived a godly life, the promise of a child had not been fulfilled.

In fact, in Luke 1:6-7 it says this:

> Both of them were righteous in the sight of God, observing all the Lord's commands and decrees blamelessly. But they were childless because Elizabeth was not able to conceive, and they were both very old.

Now, according to the Bible, Zechariah and Elizabeth were both very old. They had endured endless disappointment month after month, and they lived with a barren mentality. Their hope had been eradicated. Their waiting was no longer from a healthy place – they were overwhelmed and tired. They were just waiting for a way out of their humiliation. They could not understand why God had not heard their cry in the midst of their barrenness. Then one day everything changed. Zechariah went to work in the temple as usual; God spoke to him through an angel but Zechariah was not ready to trust. So let us continue reading their story in Luke.

> [11]While Zechariah was in the sanctuary, an angel of the Lord appeared to him, standing to the right of the incense altar. [12]Zechariah was shaken and overwhelmed with fear when he saw him. [13]But the angel said, "Don't be afraid, Zechariah! God has heard your prayer. [18]Zechariah said to the angel, "How can I be sure this will happen? I'm an old man now, and my wife is also well along in years."
>
> [19]Then the angel said, "I am Gabriel! I stand in the very presence of God. It was he who sent me to bring you this good news! [20]But now, since you didn't believe what I said, you will be silent and unable to speak until the child is born. For my words will certainly be fulfilled at the proper time."
> **— LUKE 1:11-20**

Zechariah had waited so long that even when he had an angelic visitation from Heaven, carrying a message concerning his child, he could not break out of his disappointment and habit of talking negatively. The angel is astonished and says to Zechariah, "Don't you understand, I have come from God; what I say has to be true!" But for too long Zechariah had experienced nothing. His trust and hope were gone. Unfortunately, all he was able to say came from the negative experience of his barrenness. He could not even receive the prophetic word from Heaven and so the angel silenced him.

This season of expectation could not be ruined by his negative speaking. Zechariah and Elizabeth did conceive. Elizabeth was now expectant, but Zechariah still could not speak. But once the baby was born his mouth was opened, and he made powerful declarations about the God encounters and generational blessings that would be experienced in the future. This was a new day and the barren mindset had been shifted. Hope and expectation had been reborn. Zechariah could be trusted to speak again with the right attitude. Hope had been restored.

ACTIVATION

In what areas of your life are you unable to trust and hope concerning the future? Recognise these areas and ask God to restore you by the power of His Holy Spirit.

Has your season of disappointment caused you to speak in a negative way? Do you need to write a new declaration over your life and your generations?

Ask God to heal your disappointments and write a new declaration of hope for your future.

LIVING IN EXPECTATION

Often it can feel unsafe to live life with a high level of expectation. This hopeful attitude can appear to position you in an exposed place where you just get hurt. In the Bible, hope is the anticipation of a favour filled outcome under God's direction. Hope is the confidence that grows as a result of knowing that God has guided you in the past and so you know He will lead you into your best future. Biblical hope means we base our trust firmly on what God says, with a confident expectation that He will fulfil His promises to us. It comes from a relationship with Jesus in which we know God is good and will save and help us to live our best life.

We need to understand that part of our spiritual nature is specifically created by God to live with expectation. All through the Bible we read the accounts of the prophets who awakened both the nations and individuals to their calling and destiny. Within our prophetic nature there is an expectancy of more and a looking towards the future. Our spiritual character carries a profound sense of purpose and generational legacy. We were made to dream of more beyond ourselves. All the prophets lived with this sense of expectation. Isaiah calls us to arise and shine with the glory of God and then in chapter 64, Isaiah cries out for God to rend the Heavens and come down. Habakkuk, the prophet, finds himself standing on the ramparts waiting for God to come and assures us that He will come and will not delay. Jeremiah speaks about the watchman who will proclaim the day of God's coming. He encourages us to be awake and watch as we will see the day of God's coming to the nations. Romans 8:19 reminds us that even the whole of creation is waiting in eager expectation for the children of God to be revealed. Eager expectation is one of the atmospheres of our spiritual heritage.

Being people of expectation is a natural part of our spiritual DNA. We need to understand this distinctive even when it may not come naturally to us. God designed us to be people of great expectations. He is able to provide us with a continuous supply of hope to live like this. It is not by our strength or power, but it is a gift from Him. There is a gift of grace that we need to acquire in this time of waiting: we need to wait, like creation, in eager expectation. There are many promises that will be accomplished but we need to wait to see the day of revelation. God promises us that He will pour out all the resources we need to see His promises fulfilled among us and our generations. As we read this promise in Isaiah, let us ask God to do it for us:

For I will pour out water to quench your thirst and to irrigate your parched fields. And I will pour out my Spirit on your descendants, and my blessing on your children.

— ISAIAH 44:3 (NLT)

ACTIVATION

God will pour out water into your life. Receive this refreshing.

Ask God to stir up EAGER EXPECTATION in your heart.

Ask God to awaken your prophetic sense of the "more" that is to come.

Write it down.

TIME TO EXPAND AND FLOURISH

Many of us have been through seasons when we have felt our hope has been depleted. But this is a new day and God wants to unblock the wells of hope again, those watering places in your life that remind you of the goodness of God to you and your family. Difficult days have stopped up the resource of these wells. You have felt dry and weary but God wants you to know this is a new season and you can dream again. Your hope is not hopeless but will be hope filled.

In Genesis we read that there had been a season of wells being blocked. Then a time of trouble and quarrelling ensued but, as they stood their ground and persevered, something shifted. They had been unblocking the wells. It had been tough. But suddenly the environment changed. In this verse in Genesis, we read that he moved on from there…and he dug another well.

> He moved on from there and dug another well, and no one
> quarrelled over it.
> **— GENESIS 26:22**

All around you, you have seen the limitations and restrictions of
this season, the financial, relational, work and church pressures that
have robbed your hope. However, do you realise that you were
made to flourish even in the midst of difficulty? There needs to be
an end to the quarrelling and a new trust that grows and believes
that God does know the way of life for you. God wants to awaken
your heart and asks if this can be a fresh start – a new well! I believe
there is an opportunity for growth and restoration in your life. God
wants you to move on from the barren place and dig another well
and find the water of hope. God wants you to prosper in your soul
and flourish in your life. This is your season to grow and know you
are loved and cherished. God is placing a new name over your life,
He is expanding your expectation and giving you room to dream
and flourish again.

> ...He named it Rehoboth, saying, "Now the LORD has given us
> room and we will flourish in the land."
> **— GENESIS 26:22b**

This is a promise for you: now the Lord has given us room and we
will flourish in the land! In this time of chaos and complexities, God
is giving you a time of opportunity. When it is hopeless, we can be
the carriers of expectation, dreams and purpose. There is so much
fear and uncertainty but God wants you to be confident and sure
of your future. Remember, God promises to meet with you. You
do not have to find this hope, force yourself to be hopeful, try to
conjure up any feelings of hope. This is not your responsibility! God
has promised to gift you a hope filled life. God has promised to
meet you and fill you with hope.

So now let us read this verse in Romans one more time and let the truth of these words saturate your spirit. This is your promise from God. Right now, let "the God of hope fill you with all joy and peace as you trust in him, so that you may overflow with hope by the power of the Holy Spirit." God has a plan for your life and you do not have to simply endure life, but you are made to enjoy it. You do not have to feel that you are just about surviving; God wants you to live your life hope filled and watch yourself thriving. This is a new day and time to flourish.

ACTIVATION

Ask God to show you the new wells of life and hope that He wants to reopen in your life. Can you see the God opportunities in the midst of the complexities of this season?

Ask God to help you move on from the limitations and restrictions of this season, the financial, relational, work and church pressures that have robbed your hope.

Dig a new well with God!

2

HOPE FILLED

There is hope for the tree

> "The pessimist sees difficulty in every opportunity. The optimist sees the opportunity in every difficulty."
> **— WINSTON CHURCHILL**

It is so easy for us to approach new opportunities with the cynical attitude of "is this going to last?", or "I have heard it all before", or even, "this is nothing new!". I love the quote by Winston Churchill above, challenging us to look at life from a hope filled perspective. Gordon and I live in Oxford, near to Blenheim Palace, the birthplace of Winston Churchill. You can visit this place and read excerpts of his school reports in the exhibition there. Winston was told repeatedly by his school teachers that his life would not amount to much. "This boy is not able to write or communicate adequately", was their assessment. After reading these documents, you are then led into the hall full of his books, samples of his writing and recordings of his famous speeches and finally a large display of his many honours and medals of office. Winston obviously learnt to look beyond his challenges and see them as an opportunity to grow. In the Second World War, his leadership of Britain was rooted in this simple belief: we will hope. We will never, never give up. "I will see an opportunity in the midst of our darkest hours and lead", was Winston's attitude. Like

Winston, we need to embrace this way of thinking and hope beyond what we see and celebrate each new day with eager anticipation. God is moving you into a new landscape, with new resources, and giving you room to flourish. We need to drink from this well of hope!

> [7]At least there is hope for a tree: If it is cut down, it will sprout again, and its new shoots will not fail. [8]Its roots may grow old in the ground and its stump die in the soil, [9]yet at the scent of water it will bud and put forth shoots like a plant.
> **— JOB 14:7-9**

Whatever the circumstances of the last few years, God wants you to know there is hope for you. There is hope for the tree. You may feel that your tree of life has been hacked down, pruned mercilessly, left as a shrivelled specimen struggling for life. But God promises you that even those areas that have been chopped down can sprout again. The end is not the end until God says it is the end! Much of the externals of your life may appear to have been sabotaged and ruined - but God says, "do not lose hope". There is hope for this tree. Listen again - there is hope for this tree. There is a way forward with God.

Remember in the last chapter we read this verse from Genesis:

> …and He named it Rehoboth, saying, 'Now the LORD has given us room and we will flourish in the land'.
> **— GENESIS 26:22**

God wants you to awaken your spiritual senses to discern the change of season and your ability to thrive. You are moving from a time of disputes, difficulty and quarrelling into a land where you will flourish. You may look at your life today and say there is nothing flourishing here. But I want to awaken hope and understanding. In this verse from Job that we were reading, he declares there is hope for the tree, even after a time of severe pruning, because the roots in the ground are still alive. God wants to say to you that you can flourish because you still have good roots. You may feel there is not much to show externally but, in the hidden place, you have a good root structure of heart values, prayer and spiritual investment. Hope in God! You will flourish in the land.

So what do you see and understand by this word "flourish"? You may feel you are anything but flourishing but remember our verse – there is hope for the tree. Yes, this word flourish does literally mean to grow, thrive, prosper, develop, increase and multiply. But this word flourish also carries with it an underlying understanding that for anything or anyone to flourish - that is for them to grow and develop in a healthy or vigorous way - it will happen as a result of being located in a congenial environment. In other words, your ability to flourish depends on who you are and where you are located. God wants to place you in a landscape of Rehoboth, a place where you have room for your dreams to grow: an environment of hope and a greenhouse of expectation.

You may still feel, "I do not feel I am flourishing". Maybe as you look around at your peers, your siblings and others in your friendship group, you feel you are the odd one out. Everyone else is doing well but you are still struggling relationally, financially or emotionally. But when I asked God about the significance of this word "flourish" for you in this season, He said to me, "Rachel, just remember that flourishing looks very different in different seasons". In springtime it is easy to see which plants are thriving and which are not. You can see the leafy shoots, bright green with vigorous growth. In autumn it is obvious to see which plants are flourishing, as they are the ones laden with fruit. In summer we can quickly identify the rose bushes covered with flowers, the scent of the jasmine filling the air. You can quickly see which plants are flourishing. But in winter it is not easy to see which trees are rooted well and which are not. The other seasons demonstrate their flourishing externally but in winter the flourishing takes place in the hidden place. It is all underground. This winter season is about developing a flourishing root system for this tree of hope. There is hope for the tree! In the following Psalm David expresses this same thought, so let us read:

> He will be standing firm like a flourishing tree planted by God's design, deeply rooted by the brooks of bliss, bearing fruit in every season of his life. He is never dry, never fainting, ever blessed, ever prosperous.
> — **PSALM 1:3**

You need to be careful that you do not disregard yourself because you cannot see the vibrant green in your life yet. Remember here the Psalmist talks about bearing fruit in every season of his life. I believe that God is asking you to look beyond the shoots and the fruit that you see around you and look to your own roots. Do not be distracted by other people's success. Ultimately, the health of your own roots will determine how you flourish in this next season. I believe that this revelation should stir hunger and hope in our soul. You are flourishing if you choose the atmosphere of hope and expectation and let your roots go deep into the goodness of God.

ACTIVATION

Think about our theme scripture for this chapter again: "At least there is hope for a tree: If it is cut down, it will sprout again, and its new shoots will not fail. Its roots may grow old in the ground and its stump die in the soil...".

What root systems of belief are still flourishing in the ground? Write them down.

Looking back at all the challenges of this complex year, what has been cut down?

Can you see hope for your tree of life? Speak to the roots of your life and pray.

FLOURISHING TIME

About a year ago I walked into a church in Coventry and met Sophie and her husband at a leadership day. Here is their story of hope after a long winter season.

I'm Sophie and I'm the administrator for Coventry Elim. Back on Valentine's Day of this year, yourself and Helen came to Coventry Elim and gave some training to our team. At the end of the session, you prayed and prophesied over myself and my husband, Phil, in particular praying for God to give us a child. I wanted to email you and let you know that God has been so kind and faithful to us and has gifted us with a baby boy that is due at the end of January next year, praise God. I wanted to give you a bit of context to what you prayed/prophesied into at the time as it has been such an encouragement and a testimony for this boy's life and we wanted to thank you for being obedient to God's voice and for standing with us in prayer.

We had been trying to start a family for a little while, nothing happened so we decided to get some tests. Some things had come up in these tests which we didn't fully understand at the time and had been referred to the consultant but the wait for an appointment was in 6 months' time. As we'd found out these results, we also found out we managed to conceive naturally at the same time. We were so overjoyed. We still kept that appointment but didn't think we'd need it. Sadly, we lost the first baby early on and we were pretty devastated. In your prophecy over us (which thankfully someone recorded for us), you mentioned a couple of times about weeping for a night but joy coming in the morning. This really spoke to me as when I was mis-carrying I put the song on "Your love never fails" by Jesus Culture and the lyrics are "there may be pain in the night, but joy comes in the morning". I really held onto that song and the truth of those words, so when you spoke pretty similar words over us it was a real encouragement.

The week before your prophecy we had our appointment with the consultant. He explained the test results and gave us some leaflets for treatments that we could explore to help us conceive. We came away from that meeting deciding that we were going to see how the rest of this year goes and to trust God that he will do this naturally. We'd also booked into doing further tests.

When you prayed for us, both of us felt something shift in the spirit that evening, that God had said this was enough of this season, this is what I'm promising you and it was really encouraging. I encountered the Holy Spirit so strongly on the way home physically that I hadn't experienced in years. It was also really encouraging that God had used you to show us that He has seen this whole season, He saw the many times I went on a dog walk by myself and wept before God, talking to him, not really understanding what was going on and that He cares and He loves me; He is so kind. We had renewed hope and faith for this new season.

We had further tests and had another appointment and miraculously these results came back clear; we were stunned. Another answer to prayer! A couple of months later we managed to conceive naturally and here we are now, half way through this pregnancy, with a healthy baby boy and the whole pregnancy has gone so smoothly. God has been so kind to us. We also found out that as of January next year, Phil's work have changed their paternity policy and he's able to take nearly 6 months full pay at the start of our family life together. Again another sign of God's goodness and kindness to us and the timing of it is just incredible, as if the baby were due before January he wouldn't have been entitled to it.

I know that this will change your percentage rates as you told us there was a high percentage of girls that are conceived after you pray - haha! But thank you so much for standing with us. I've listened to the prayer/prophecy multiple times throughout the pregnancy so far as it really grounds me every time I've felt a bit nervous. Please feel free to share this testimony with others who are in a similar situation to help hope arise in them, because if He's done it for us, He can do it for them too.

There is hope for the tree. Even when the roots are old in the ground and it seems that it is impossible, God has a plan!

EXPECTATION – THE SCENT OF WATER

[7]At least there is hope for a tree: If it is cut down, it will sprout again, and its new shoots will not fail. [8]Its roots may grow old in the ground and its stump die in the soil, [9]yet at the scent of water it will bud and put forth shoots like a plant.

— JOB 14:7-9

Can you smell the scent of water? Is hope arising? In this season, God is awakening your spiritual eyes, ears and senses to be aware of what He is doing in your life. Can you smell this scent of water? Can you discern the new hope arising in your spirit?

As a child, from the age of three to sixteen, I grew up in Mumbai as the daughter of missionary parents. Every May we knew it would be hot, very hot, at least forty degrees centigrade and humid. The heat would get more and more intense until we were all longing for rain and the arrival of the monsoon. We knew the date that rain would come and usually by the 20th of June we were all preparing for the final release from the hot, sticky days. But before we felt the rain on our faces, we could smell it. It would be hot but suddenly you could smell the scent of water in the acrid, dusty air. The scent of rain. A cry would go up in the neighbourhood, "Run, the rain is coming, I can smell it." You usually had a few minutes before the breeze intensified and suddenly there was the sound of heavy rain.

Can you recognise these rain clouds touching your life? Are you aware of hope and fresh faith being released? I believe that God wants to awaken your spiritual senses too so that you are able to discern the scent of water bringing life to your circumstances. There is hope for the tree. There is another part of the story that is waiting to be written in your life.

This last winter had a dire effect on my garden. Once springtime arrived, I realised that I had lost ten mature shrubs; each one had a different place of affection in my heart. They had all been gifts representing different seasons of our life: special birthdays, wedding anniversaries and other special events. But one in particular grieved me – it was the sorry state of my olive tree. This had been a gift to me for my ministry in St Aldates, Oxford, and had grown in our front garden. But now this tree looked lifeless. However, one day while reading this scripture from Job, I wondered if there was hope for my olive tree. Would it, too, sprout again at the scent of water? So I decided to give the tree time. I left it in the ground. Although it looked dead and all the branches had dropped their leaves and were brown and brittle, I decided to water this tree. I began to take a bucket of water every three to four days and drench the roots with the water. At first the leaves continued to drop and the frail branches snapped off but then something began to change. I began to remove what was obviously dead but discovered some of the branches were beginning to turn green and become flexible again. Fresh sap was starting to rise. After continuing for another six weeks, buds began to form and now I have one branch that is full of leaves, even with flowers, and my tree may even fruit this fall.

The tree that now stands in my front garden has a different shape and structure: there is still plenty of evidence of the dead branches, but there is hope for this tree. I continue to saturate these roots with water and my tree has begun to sprout. I had lost all hope for this tree but, at the scent of water, it has sprouted again!

I believe that God wants you, too, to take a moment and look at the garden of your life. Maybe there are areas that have experienced the harsh effects of a brutal winter but, at the scent of water, there is hope for the tree. Take a moment with God and ask Him to show you how to awaken with His Holy Spirit what looks to have died. Can you discern the water of life and stir hope once again?

ACTIVATION

Can you "smell" the presence of God in your life? Ask God to give you a strategy to find that scent of water that you need in your life.

Can you see the first cracks of breakthrough in your world? Let this scent of hope awaken fresh shoots. Ask God to soak the roots of your life with His water.

As you pray, awaken your spiritual senses to His plans today. He holds the timing and your days in His hands. Lean into God and trust Him.

GOD ENCOUNTERS

Living in India taught me that, in a moment, life can change for the better. One moment you were just about surviving in stifling heat, everyone was exhausted, and then suddenly, in the next second, the rain came and everything changed. In just a matter of days the dead, dry grass became green on the sides of the roads. People were calmer and life had hope again. The rain had come. Food would grow, the markets would be full of produce. We had survived a time of intense heat once again.

It is similar in our spiritual lives too. We need to recognise that, when we become desperate, these feelings of frustration and our anxieties are just a symptom of our inner hunger and thirst for God. We can feel the intense heat of our trials and adversities. We feel agitated and on edge and often try to distract ourselves from these emotions by getting absorbed in activities. However, the tensions only increase and we need to recognise that these stresses are really rooted in a need for time with God. The Psalmist, David, expresses his weariness like this:

> My soul thirsts for God, for the living God. When can I go and meet with God?
> — **PSALM 42:2**

Maybe you are asking similar questions to the psalmist. Where can I go to meet with God? I believe that there are times, places and spaces where we can smell that scent of water more easily. As we discussed earlier in this chapter, when looking at the conditions for flourishing, we noticed that true flourishing depended on where you were placed as well as what you did with your life. There are atmospheres that attract the rain of God. As we position ourselves with an attitude of desperation - hunger - humility - obedience - sacrifice - generosity (and many other life choices), we find we do meet with God. But sometimes it is not so much about making the right internal choices of our heart but simply finding a quiet space where you can relax. Where do you need to go to meet with God? I find that I often need to disconnect from the demands of all my responsibilities for a few hours. I need to switch off my phone, quieten my mind and just let the true depth of my cry come before God. It takes courage to be still and let the roots of your being enter the presence of God. In this quiet place of reflection, God will water your soul. God will speak to you. Remember there is hope for this tree and, at the scent of water, life will sprout again. Ideas, possibilities and dreams that have seemed dead in the ground will sprout again as they are irrigated by the water of His presence. Our feelings of hopelessness can be answered after just one meeting with God.

HOPE FILLED FUTURE

You need to know that God has good plans for your life. He wants to affirm you and encourage you. We are often so reluctant to take the time and create the space to listen to God. Jeremiah, the prophet, reassures us, in the following well-known passage of scripture, that God wants to speak to us. Let us read these verses:

> [11]"For I know the plans I have for you", declares the LORD, "plans to prosper you and not to harm you, plans to give you hope and a future. [12]Then you will call on me and come and pray to me, and I will listen to you."
> **— JEREMIAH 29:11-12**

Here Jeremiah inspires us that God wants to speak to us. He has good plans, full of hope, to share with us but we need to make the time to come and pray and listen to Him. All of us have a receptor in the internal being of our lives, specially designed by God, that enables us to hear Him. If you will prepare a space, God will speak to you and encourage you with plans of hope about your future.

We have considered the scripture about hope for the tree from the book of Job. Job had a tough life and knew what it was to be overwhelmed by his circumstances and almost lose hope. He lost his health, his wealth and his family, and even his friends were not very supportive. Yet we read in the book of Job that he found time to pray for his friends and discovered God had a plan to give him back double for all his trouble. Here is the passage in Job for you to read:

> ¹⁰After Job had prayed for his friends, the LORD restored his fortunes and gave him twice as much as he had before. ¹¹All his brothers and sisters and everyone who had known him before came and ate with him in his house. They comforted and consoled him over all the trouble the LORD had brought on him, and each one gave him a piece of silver and a gold ring. ¹²The LORD blessed the latter part of Job's life more than the former part.
> — **JOB 42:10-12**

So, after Job prayed for his friends, God returned double of everything that he had had previously, and his life turned around. In fact, this scripture says that this latter part of his life experienced a greater blessing. There is hope for the tree. Job knew what he was talking about when he wrote this scripture for us to read. When everything felt as though it was finished, Job discovered that God had a plan of hope for him.

All through history we read the stories of amazing people who discovered how to find hope in God in their times of trouble. Corrie ten Boom experienced the atrocities of the concentration camps during the Second World War. She lost her family, was persecuted for being a Jew, and watched her friends and sister being tortured but still kept her eyes on God. The Nazi soldiers robbed her of everything she owned, tried to take her dignity and freedom, but her faith stood strong. She kept her hope and trust in God. This famous quote of hers is still an inspiration to us today:

"Never be afraid to trust an unknown future to a known God."
— **CORRIE TEN BOOM**

So, however difficult life has been, remember there is hope for the tree. God has good plans for your life so press in and let God stir your hope and dreams once again. Trust your future to God and watch what happens!

ACTIVATION

What plans do you need God to speak to you about?

What are the practical adjustments you need to make to create a meeting place with God. Write these down.

Now take time to pray and listen and then receive God's hope filled plans for your life.

3

HOPE FILLED

In the face of delay and disappointment

> "Hope is not blind optimism. It's not ignoring the enormity of the task ahead, or the roadblocks that stand in our path. It's not sitting on the side-lines or shirking from a fight. Hope is that thing inside us that insists, despite all the evidence to the contrary, that something better awaits us if we have the courage to reach for it, work for it, and believe for it."
> **— BARACK OBAMA**

Is hope a dangerous emotion? Some would say it is better not to hope and in so doing protect yourself from the pain of terrible disappointment. But, as we have already discussed, we do not have this option. Hope is a God-given attribute and God says it must remain as a foundational part of our character. So how do we handle life when it feels more hopeless than hope filled? It requires great courage to live this hope filled life. Adversities do come. Our hope ridicules us and we are challenged to the very core of our trust. But hope must remain. How?

EVEN IF IT KILLS ME – I WILL HOPE

We have been reading the story of the life of Job and his courageous stand in the midst of trouble. He found the scent of water, the promise of hope, even when his life had been cut to the core and he had lost everything. He believed there was hope for his tree. His friends were all trying to correct his thinking and challenge his attitudes but he would not downsize his hope and expectations of God. In this scripture we read his courageous statement of hope:

> "Though he slay me, yet will I hope in him; I will surely defend my ways to his face."
> — **JOB 13:15**

Job would not be moved. He could not let go. You can hear him scream this truth to himself, and anyone listening, through all his troubles, "I have to trust God. Even if my hope in God kills me, I will still hope in Him." Many of us will recognise this watershed moment where we find ourselves standing at the crossroads of life and our hope in God appears to be taunting us; everything is shouting, "you will fail", but you know you have to trust in God. This is raw courage. This is trust!

Unfortunately, it seems we all need to navigate this challenge of life sometime. There will be a moment when suddenly all your hopes and dreams collide and then they seem to turn and mock you, but you have to make the bold decision to stand and trust God. It is not easy but it is necessary.

HUMILIATED BY HOPE – NEARLY

My hope in God appeared to humiliate me. I was now 36 weeks pregnant, carrying our second child, and I needed a miracle. Gordon and I were living in Nairobi and we were working with Christ for all Nations (CfaN) and Reinhard Bonnke. We were seeing signs and wonders all around us every day but at home it was tough. We needed money for bills, in fact for one bill in particular. My medical bill for the antenatal care and birth of this baby. This bill was unexpected and larger than we had anticipated. Each month we trusted God to provide our needs and all the general bills were covered but this bill was still outstanding. There was just no surplus cash. Once again I was attending my antenatal appointment without the money to confirm and pay for my birthing arrangements. I dreaded walking into the clinic that day. The smiling receptionist greeted me, "Mrs Hickson, you are looking well, and the baby is coming soon. Have you confirmed and paid for your birthing needs? It is getting close now and we need to finalise this bill." I swallowed hard and stumbled to find my words. "I am sorry", I answered, "we still do not have the cash to pay this bill yet. As soon as it arrives in our account, I will bring it to you. We do want to confirm the birth of our baby here in Nairobi hospital." "Well you need to do this urgently now, Mrs Hickson, time is getting short", she replied. "Yes, I know, I will try", I replied helplessly. Yet again I had hoped and here I was looking at nothing. "God, I have trusted you and this is now urgent", I said quietly. I was standing at the crossroads of trust and felt humiliated. I wondered if I should ask for help. Should I phone the Christ for all Nations office and ask for a loan? I knew that they were generous and would help. But I felt God had asked us to trust Him and live by faith while we were serving in Africa. We were not receiving a salary but people generously supported us with gifts and donations at various times. Our general expenses were always covered on time, and easily, and so I had not expected this maternity bill to be a struggle; but now it was a crisis of trust.

I suddenly remembered that Peter Vandenberg, one of the CfaN team, was visiting us the next day and coming to our home. Maybe he would bring the money and he would be the answer. I cooked a good meal, we chatted together, and Peter even asked about the baby and the pregnancy. The next day we dropped him at the airport but he had not given us any money. This was my last hope. How would I pay this bill? I had stood in the kitchen at breakfast time that morning, toying with the idea of asking Peter for a CfaN loan for the bill but had had no peace, and so I had let the moment go. Now he had left and I had no plan B. Then to make matters worse, the clinic had sent a letter that morning in the post, confirming all my birthing details with the final bill giving me a deadline of just three days' time. This bill had to be paid.

I did not sleep much that night. Gordon and I had prayed, hoped, waited and it seemed my trust would humiliate me. I decided to go to the clinic and be honest and ask them for help. However, on my way to the clinic I needed to go to the CfaN office first and drop off some accounts. As I entered the office, the secretary called me, "Oh Rachel, I am glad you are here, there is a telex for you. Reinhard has sent you a message." I opened the note and read the letter. It read as follows: "I just wanted you to know that I was ministering in Switzerland and I showed the video of the Malawi Miracle, where you were the campaign directors. After the meeting, a man came to me and asked that I send you a gift urgently for the sum of 2,000 Swiss Francs. Please take this money from the CfaN account and use it for your needs. Reinhard Bonnke." I was stunned. I sat down and cried. The financial department gave me the cash immediately, and I left the office with the money, tears streaming down my face.

This time I walked into the clinic with a smile too. "Ah, Mrs Hickson", the smiling receptionist greeted me once again, "have you come to settle your bill?" "Yes, I have!", I replied with joy, "The money has come!". I paid the outstanding bills and still had a little surplus. "Have you got everything ready for your baby now?", the receptionist asked. Suddenly I realised I had money for my dreams too. I had wanted to go and buy some toys, clothes and essentials for this baby's arrival. I went to the shops and shopped! Once finished

I had just a little change left in my hands and a happy heart. This gift had covered everything. God had rescued me. David, my son, was born just two days later. He arrived early and everything was paid in full – just in time!

CHOOSE HOPE

Handling these difficult delay issues in your walk with God requires grace. It expands your courage. You go on a journey of trust and learn to understand God's time schedules and how He fulfills His promises. Remember, hope must remain – and learning how to keep your hope healthy during delay becomes a battle for your beliefs. But it is a battle we need to learn to win. So many become disheartened and bitter in the battle. We need to remember that our hope is not just an emotional wishing for something, but a hope which is spiritual, born from a God-inspired revelation. Our hope is a God-given desire for something with a divine, hope filled expectation of accomplishment. We need to learn how to hold fast to our hope, even in the midst of delays and disappointments.

In Proverbs we read about the two responses we can have during these times of waiting:

> Hope deferred makes the heart sick, but a longing fulfilled is a tree of life.
> **— PROVERBS 13:12**

Often we only quote the first part of this verse, "Hope deferred makes the heart sick", and we forget the second part of the verse which states, "but a longing fulfilled is the tree of life". This verse illustrates for us the two alternative outcomes in our battle for hope. These are the two common reactions we can have: either it is disappointment that brings emotional pain and can eventually make the heart sick and bitter, or it is hope that knows that this delay is only temporary and breakthrough will come, bringing the promise, resulting in a fulfilled life. Today we need to find courage and believe that even in the delay there is a path of life. Choose the path of life.

ACTIVATION

How have you handled the seasons of delay in your life?

Are there areas where your heart is wounded? Have you felt humiliated? Ask God to heal the weariness and pain.

Ask God to restore your trust so that, like Job, you can hope in God.

Write down the hope challenges you have at this time and surrender them to God. Decide to trust. Choose to hope and ask God to help you.

HOLDING FAST TO TRUE HOPE

But why the delays? Are they necessary? We need a renewed understanding of what it means to have spiritual hope rather than simply a positive outlook. Our hope is not just an optimistic worldview. Our hope is different from optimism. Our hope is not a set of self-help techniques and positive thinking. Our hope is not based on chance or fantasy. Our hope is different from false hope or presumption. Our hope originates in a word from God, spoken to us to catalyse our faith to believe for more. This hope has a Kingdom dynamic. As such, our hope does not just operate in the natural realm of our everyday world, but it has spiritual repercussions against the devil too. So the battle to maintain our hope is not just us dealing with our natural insecurities and sense of failure but it is also about resisting the devil and his desire to rob us of our hope. In the book of Daniel, we read the story of his wrestle in the place of prayer:

> [12]Then he continued, "Do not be afraid, Daniel. Since the first day that you set your mind to gain understanding and to humble yourself before your God, your words were heard, and I have come in response to them. [13]But the prince of the Persian kingdom resisted me twenty-one days."
> — **DANIEL 10:12-13**

So why these delays? It is not the reluctance of God to act but rather it is about waiting for the correct alignment between Heaven and earth for the breakthrough to happen. In the verses above, we read that God acted on Daniel's behalf from the moment that Daniel's prayers were heard in Heaven but there was demonic resistance for 21 days! We need to understand that because our hope is a spiritual hope, we are involved in a spiritual wrestle. This is a real struggle that requires our courage to stand, wait and trust.

The battleground for our hope usually plays out in the following areas of our lives. We contend for our hope concerning our relationships, whether family or friends, our health, our finances and wealth, and for our purpose and future. We have dreams, plans, hopes that we carry deep within us, and they are activated in our conversations with God. These hopes are developed in the secret place of our friendship with Him. Our aspirations are birthed in prayer as we discover God's plans for our lives. We are inspired by these spiritual, God-breathed ideas. Our hope is stirred. So often the battle for our hope then begins. We need to remind ourselves this hope is based on Jesus and His word spoken to us. True hope is not just a good idea, it is a God idea. The Bible speaks about our hope like this:

> We have this hope as an anchor for the soul, firm and secure. It enters the inner sanctuary behind the curtain.
> — **HEBREWS 6:19**

> Now faith is the substance of things hoped for, the evidence of things not seen.
> **— HEBREWS 11:1 (KJV)**

So we need to let the word of God change our way of thinking. We need to rehearse these truths and challenge any "stinking thinking" that has become lodged in our hearts. We must dream again, expressing our unfiltered God-given desires, and walk this journey of true hope, allowing it to awaken our expectation, trigger our faith and deepen our love for God. This is a new season and a new day and God wants you to write down and mark this day as the day you kickstarted your fresh adventure of hope.

ACTIVATION

Sit and take a moment with God, and listen.

Ask God to remind you of unexpected encounters that filled you with hope.

Remember those times where God activated your dreams and inspired you.

Write them down.

Now take a moment and recognise the battles of hope you have experienced.

Write them down.

Take a moment to pray and trust that God hears you, just as he heard Daniel.

LONG TERM DELAYS

When our hope enters a season of long-term delay, it challenges the foundation of our courage, perseverance and ability to trust. We can feel many mixed emotions and often the reasons are hard to explain. Maybe you can identify with the child in the following story:

There was a boy waiting at the bus stop for his dad. Just before he had left home that morning, his dad had promised him that he would be there to collect him from the bus that day. Once school finished, the lad clambered onto the bus, all excited. His expectation was high. His dad had promised to be at the bus stop and walk him home. The bus stop soon came into view but the boy could not see his dad. He stepped off the bus and decided to wait. His dad would come any minute. He watched the road, trying to see if he could see his dad coming. But, after ten minutes, no one had come. Now the excitement started to fade; his head dropped and he choked back his tears of disappointment. Another ten minutes. Still no one. Now he felt angry. "Where is dad?", he wanted to shout, as he began to pace up and down the road near to the bus stop. Still no dad. Now confusion. What should he do? Should he go home as normal and just forget that his dad had ever promised to collect him? Should he wait? Another ten minutes elapsed. Now he felt fear. What had happened? Where was dad? A mixture of emotions churned in his stomach: fear, confusion, anger but the excitement had gone. Finally, he walked home dejected. Thirty minutes later dad walked through the door. "I went to the bus stop but you were gone. I am so sorry I was late. I am here now." The boy barely lifted his face; he was too confused and emotionally drained. His dad continued, "there was a problem at work. I was delayed. I tried to come on time." But the boy was too distracted by the pain he felt to ask any questions. He knew his dad was here now. Dad had gone to the bus stop, albeit 45 minutes late, but the moment of hope for this boy had passed. Many years later, when reflecting on that day, this little boy realised that this had been the day that his dad's boss had collapsed at work with a heart attack and then later died. As a nine-year-old boy he had not understood the reason for this delay; he had been hurt. Now years later, with retrospective understanding, he realised that his dad had made it to the bus stop, even if 45 minutes late. His dad had moved heaven and earth to be there. As a boy he had not been forgotten, abandoned or considered second class by his dad. But at just nine years old he had not appreciated the bigger picture of life that had been at play on that day. He only saw the circumstances through the myopic lenses of his childish expectations that had been dashed.

Many times we are like this little boy in the story. We do not have the wisdom to understand the reasons for the delay in that moment. But often, when we take time to look back, we can recognise the fingerprints of God and realise that we were not forgotten or abandoned by God either. In these perplexing times we need to ask God to show us the bigger picture. We need to learn to look beyond ourselves and see what God is doing. In these times of delay, we need to embrace the word of God, stand firm, and look to the fuller perspective. As we read the Psalms, we find that, again and again, David has to remind himself that his hope is secure in God. Let us read some of these scriptures:

> But now, Lord, what do I look for? My hope is in you.
> — **PSALM 39:7**

> Why are you downcast, O my soul? Why so disturbed within me? Put your hope in God, for I will yet praise him, my Saviour and my God.
> — **PSALM 42:5, 11**

When we experience hardship, our natural emotional default is to fear, get depressed and doubt. Our circumstances will always try to unsettle our soul and pull us down. So where will we turn? Look to God and study His word. These seasons of delay need to develop a resolute diligence in us and an unshakable belief in God's word. So remind yourself of these scriptures. They are our battle weapons!

> Remember the word to your servant, for you have given me hope.
> — **PSALM 119:49**

> [11]We want each of you to show this same diligence to the very end, in order to make your hope sure…[18]God did this so that, by two unchangeable things in which it is impossible for God to lie, we who have fled to take hold of the hope offered to us may be greatly encouraged. [19]We have this hope as an anchor for the soul, firm and secure. It enters the inner sanctuary behind the curtain.
> — **HEBREWS 6:11, 18-19**

> [35]So do not throw away your confidence; it will be richly rewarded. [36]You need to persevere so that when you have done the will of God, you will receive what he has promised. [37]For in just a very little while, "He who is coming will come and will not delay. But my righteous one will live by faith. And if he shrinks back, I will not be pleased with him." But we are not of those who shrink back and are destroyed, but of those who believe and are saved.
> — **HEBREWS 10:35-37**

ACTIVATION

Take a moment to read and then re-read these scriptures.

Hope in God and His word. Ask God to restore your confidence.

Ask God to show you His perspective in your season of delays. Can you see the fingerprints of God retrospectively in those seasons of delay?

Thank God that He has never abandoned you.

PAINFUL DISAPPOINTMENTS

We must deal with the pain of any wounded hope effectively. Any hopes and dreams that have been delayed and any disappointments hidden in our hearts can damage our confidence to hope again. When hope encounters these trials of delay and disappointment, our absolute trust in God's reliability and goodness is shaken. So we need to process these events with honesty and talk to God and find peace. Disappointment is literally the pain of enduring a "missed appointment". You had hoped for a baby; waited to be married; wanted to move to a new house; needed to change your job; and you had set a time in your heart, believing and hoping that God would answer, and then nothing happened.

The Bible says if we hope in God we will not be disappointed. But this can seem very confusing when you are carrying the pain of recent disappointment in your life. So what does the Bible mean? We find these scriptures in Isaiah and then in Romans as quoted below:

> ...those who hope in me will not be disappointed.
> **— ISAIAH 49:23**

...and this hope does not disappoint us, because God has poured out his love into our hearts by the Holy Spirit, whom he has given us.

— **ROMANS 5:2-5**

Why then is the pain of our disappointment so real if the Bible says we will not be disappointed? The reason is this: the Bible promises that we will not experience disappointment if we keep our hope God focussed. When we hope in God, we will not be disappointed. Somehow, even while believing for new doors to open or different opportunities to develop, we must keep our hope rooted in God and not in the circumstance we desire. People and projects always have the potential to disappoint us but hope, truly rooted in God, will not fail. Our challenge is to stay connected in our relationships, and have great hope for our health, finances and future, knowing that, even if people fail us, God is in control and our hope is secure. This is a trust challenge for our minds and hearts. Whatever the doubts and fears we need to conquer or the various disappointments we may experience, we must see beyond the circumstances and know that our hope in God is secure and will not fail.

A MISSED APPOINTMENT OR NOT?

I sat at my desk heartbroken, trying to process the full repercussions of the phone call I had just received. We had lost the house. It was final. As I reflected on the last six months, it was so confusing. We had been so confident that God had led us to this place and everything seemed perfect. We had been so full of hope and expectation that this was the right place and all our prayers had seemed to confirm this. Then, more recently, things had started to go wrong. The letters and phone calls with the solicitor had become vaguer. A date of sale could not be confirmed and the buyers kept giving us various excuses, but we had kept hoping. We had started to feel uneasy ourselves about a month before but dismissed these fears quickly as just nerves. God would help us, we were sure. But here I sat full of disappointment. It was confirmed: we had lost this house. Why, God? Surely this was the right one; we had even felt God had asked us to move. This moment felt like brutal betrayal. I was so confused.

A year later, here I was reflecting on the memory of that terrible day and now I was smiling. I could still see myself sitting at that desk devastated and angry. It had felt like the end of the world when we lost this house of our hopes and dreams. But life had continued, hope had been more than fulfilled, and now I was living in the best city ever. I recalled the deep feelings of disappointment and anger of that day and the weeks afterwards. Why did God not help us in those moments when we lost the house that we had wanted?

But a year later my perspective of that moment had radically shifted. I had been convinced God had failed me that day, but today I could see how God had led us to a better place of greater blessing. We had been in a season of transition and, although the final destination had changed, this process of our lost house had been a significant part of our story. As we had pursued the first house, it had also begun to shift our attitudes about where we were going to be living. The house we were looking at was in Peterborough. We had felt that God had asked us to leave Watford, where we had been ministering for the last 17 years, and move to work with Dave and Karen Smith at Kingsgate Church. We were excited and this house was perfect. But then this door had shut and we continued to house hunt. We looked at 40 properties in Peterborough but none of them seemed right and we had no peace. We were perplexed. Maybe we should just give up and stay in Watford but somehow the house hunting had shifted our heart connections locally and we now wanted to move. We had a great couple, Tim and Helen Roberts, who were ready to lead the churches and we had already transitioned to them. So our job was done. We felt disconnected in Watford and were homeless in Peterborough. Where was God?

At this time, David, our son, was looking at universities for the next season of his life. He was studying Maths and Business and had an Open Day in Oxford to consider their courses. Gordon decided to go with him. Having dropped David at the college for the weekend, Gordon took the opportunity to meet with friends in the town. On the Sunday morning he stayed and went to church with them at St Aldates, Oxford. Here we met old friends from Paris, Charlie and Anita Cleverly. Charlie was now the Rector of St Aldates. After the service they invited Gordon to lunch and, out of the blue, offered him a job as the Parish Vicar of St Aldates. They had just advertised for the job but had not had a suitable applicant apply. When they heard we were planning to move from Watford, they asked us to consider Oxford. When Gordon phoned me, everything in my spirit leapt. It was not Peterborough, it was Oxford! Within three months we had arrived. Gordon had taken up his role. I was living in the church house and we were content. God had opened miraculous doors of favour for Gordon to be ordained into the Anglican Church, and we were now looking for our own house in Oxford. This time everything went smoothly. We completed our house purchase in just four weeks from viewing to moving in and everything was perfect. In fact, we still live in Oxford today.

With hindsight, I can see how the faithful hand of God had led us on this journey from Watford, to Peterborough, to Oxford. God had needed to first uproot us from Watford, and our deep relationships of over twenty-five years, and prepare us for a move. He had used Peterborough as a stepping stone on this path. We had fallen in love with the Peterborough house and in our hearts had left Watford. But this door had closed. At the time when we were looking in Peterborough, the job in Oxford did not exist. Charlie and Anita were not in post, and they had no need for a minister.

So God prepared us ahead of time for a quick move. When Gordon walked into St Aldates on that Sunday morning, he was ready to move. The heartbreak of Peterborough had prepared us for this!

Over the years I have learnt that, so often what we consider as the missed appointments of God, are just part of his stepping stones in the planning of our life. I thought God had utterly failed me but now I realise that it was all a timing issue. God was preparing my heart for a move but had to get me ready in another field before He could open the next door of destiny in our lives. This disappointment was all about timing. I thought God had missed His appointment with me and failed me. But now I understand that I had missed God's purpose in the plan and He had led me. God had a plan and he was trustworthy. I just could not understand the path we were navigating! We can so often feel that God has abandoned us in the wilderness without care when, in actual fact, He has been leading us to a new land through some difficult terrain.

A DOOR OF HOPE

This whole area of the goodness of God is difficult to explain and usually only fully understood once you have experienced it for yourself. Somehow the incredible love of God is able to persuade us and teach us to trust, even in the midst of great trouble and hardship. God is able to woo us with His love. The prophet Hosea speaks about a door of hope, opened in the valley of trouble. Hosea had a difficult life. He was asked by God to marry a woman who was a prostitute. He pursued his wife with his love, even though she remained constantly unfaithful to him. In fact, Hosea was enacting a prophetic illustration of how God's love for us is relentless, even when we are unfaithful. We read this passage in Hosea:

> [14]Therefore I am now going to allure her; I will lead her into the wilderness and speak tenderly to her [15]There I will give her

back her vineyards, and will make the Valley of Achor a door of hope. There she will respond as in the days of her youth, as in the day she came up out of Egypt. [16]"In that day," declares the LORD, you will call me 'my husband'; you will no longer call me 'my master'."

— HOSEA 2:14-16

Here the Valley of Achor can be translated as the valley of trouble. God is calling you out of the valley of disappointment and delay and speaking tenderly to you. He wants you to be aware of His love as He leads you out of this wilderness season and opens a door of hope for you. There is a door of hope. You may feel so much has been stripped and stolen but God has a plan of restoration for your life. God is speaking into your life today, "There is a door of hope for you!". God wants your relationship to change from a working one, where He is the boss and master, to a relational one where you know Him intimately as your friend and lover. If you hope in your God, you will not be disappointed. He has a way of hope for you again. So walk through this door of hope.

ACTIVATION

Is there disappointment and grief that holds your heart? Can you look back at those missed appointments and ask God to show you His timing and plans in the story today? Can you give these situations to God? Name them and write them down.

Now ask God to show you the door of hope.

Ask Him to lead you through this door, leaving the valley of trouble behind you.

Remember, Jesus is the DOOR of life.

Now walk out from the valley of trouble and through the door of hope. God will put a fresh anointing upon you, a new spirit within your heart, and renew your hope. He will remove the old sense of failure and depression and heal the battle scars of yesterday. Take some time to reflect with God and understand those valleys of trouble, and ask God to show you where He was standing in that journey. You were not alone or abandoned. Are you ready to hope again? God will refresh you with a new vision and new hope. Let this scripture be your prayer as you look to Him and wait:

But as for me, I watch in hope for the LORD, I wait for God my Saviour; my God will hear me.
— MICAH 7:7

4

HOPE FILLED

For my health and emotional wellbeing

> "We must accept finite disappointment, but we must never lose infinite hope."
> — **MARTIN LUTHER KING**

I walked into the kitchen and a statement on the wall confronted me, "It is well with my soul!". A statement of hope, life and wellbeing. At that time, I was not sure how my soul was faring. I was physically tired after a long flight, emotionally drained after walking with a close friend through various cancer scares, and needing to know God was tangibly present to help me. But this bold declaration of hope lifted me. I found hope – it was well with my soul, God had promised me that. Suddenly scriptures and promises raced through my mind, all assuring me that God would help me. I was okay, life ahead was going to be great. Yes, I would turn my attention and focus on God. Just as this scripture encourages us:

> But as for me, I watch in hope for the LORD, I wait for God my Saviour; my God will hear me.
> — **MICAH 7:7**

In the previous chapters we have unpacked the definition of hope and its challenges and confirmed that we are called to live hope filled lives. As the quote above by Martin Luther King states, our disappointments are temporary, but our hope is long lasting, even eternal. In these next chapters, I now want to explore how we practically live hope filled in the different spheres of our life. We have already discussed that our challenges of hope are usually in the areas of our relationships, whether family or friends; in our health; in our finances and wealth; and in grasping our sense of purpose for the future. We have also agreed that this hope is not just a set of mantras and sayings that we use to convince ourselves that life is good. No, the foundation of our hope is based on our relationship with God who describes and secures our hope filled life for us. So, firstly, I want to examine this area of health and wellbeing. Why can we have hope that God will take care of our body, mind and soul? Is this a realistic expectation? Time to explore a hope filled, vibrant life but let me start with my own story of hope.

I SHALL NOT DIE – BUT LIVE

In 1984 my husband, Gordon, and I had just arrived in Zimbabwe to work alongside evangelist, Reinhard Bonnke, in his Christ for all Nations ministry. I was twenty-four years old at the time and was naively determined that we were going to be "the men and women of power for the hour", here to change the nation. But just six weeks later I was involved in a serious road traffic accident, as mentioned in Chapter One, and was fighting for my life.

It was the 27 October 1984 and we had been conducting large outreach gatherings in Harare. About 25,000 people had attended the meeting on this particular evening and we had seen God working in miraculous ways. Leaving the meeting, we had just arrived home when we heard the sound of a serious car accident right outside our house. We arrived at the scene and discovered that several ministers of President Mugabe's government had been injured in the accident. Immediately we got involved and began administering first aid to the injured. But while I was busy attending to the crushed people inside the car, a seven-ton military truck came down the hill towards the traffic lights outside our home and ploughed into the stationary vehicles. Suddenly I realised what was happening, but it was too late to escape and I was crushed between this truck and the cars. Everything from my hips down was crushed in the impact and both my legs were broken in many different places. Having stopped to help people injured in a car crash, I now found myself in an ambulance being rushed to a hospital in Harare.

Initially it seemed that my severely fractured bones in both legs were my main problem. My legs were set in plaster and I was told they would take three to four months to heal, during which time I would be confined to a wheelchair. Nicola, my daughter, was just six months old at this time and I wondered how on earth I was going to cope looking after her while in my wheelchair. But, just twelve hours later, a serious complication set in and being in a wheelchair became the least of my troubles – I was fighting for my life. Sometimes, when a bone is broken, fat tissue can seep into the blood stream causing a fat embolism. This fat then travels through the blood stream, through the lungs, heart and up into the brain stem causing a life-threatening condition. Unfortunately, I began to have multiple fat emboli and slipped into a coma. As I fell into this deep coma, the medical staff were increasingly concerned by my lack of response after three days. Then a scan revealed that there was extensive brain damage to my brain stem region and they expected me to die. Word was sent to my family in the UK to come to my bedside to say farewell.

This may sound strange but I am grateful in so many ways that such a terrible accident happened to me in Zimbabwe and not in England, my home nation. Any English person would no doubt think they would be better off in England where there is better medical care.

But no, I was happy it happened in Africa where they have better miracle care! In Africa the people are not afraid to passionately get hold of God for hours and pray with strong authority: "No! Rachel will not die. She will live." And that is exactly what they did. Despite the fact that I had only been in Africa for six short weeks and they hardly knew me, I later discovered that five churches across Harare joined together to storm heaven night and day until God restored me to health. Twenty-four hours a day there were never less than a thousand people praying for God to do a miracle!

There was also a wonderful girl called Linda, who had only been saved three months. She had been working in the office with me sorting decision cards each morning after the altar calls each night. We had chatted about many things over the hours and, when she heard the news of my accident, she rushed to my bedside. Still a very young Christian, she did not know her Bible very well but she had great confidence in its power to heal. So she took the Bible and began to read out every scripture she could find onto a tape recorder. Once she had recorded her tape, she placed it in a walk-man, like an iPod, and played these scriptures to me in my coma. She was so committed that she stayed with me 24 hours a day, sometimes sleeping under my bed, so that she made sure the tape was turned each time one side was completed. During this process, the nursing staff came to remove me from my bed for further tests. As they removed the walk-man, the machine monitoring my vital signs suddenly began to beep loudly. In a panic, the nurse cried, "replace the walk-man, she needs that tape to stay alive!". Without understanding, they had acknowledged the power of the Word of God. In fact, I was told later that they were so impacted by the power the tape had to bring me life that they spoke to Gordon, my husband, and he was able to finally bring the radiographer to faith in Jesus. There is power in the Word!

As quickly as they were able, my parents arrived in Harare and rushed to my bedside. My Dad, being a man of great faith, stood at the end of my bed and read out the following declaration based on Psalm 118:17-18:

> "Rachel, you shall not die but live for the Lord, and you will proclaim that which is within you. For God has chastened you severely but has not given you over to death."

Somehow that was a turning point for my life because, five hours later, I woke up totally compos mentis. God had healed me. I still had two broken legs but He had healed me from the life-threatening emboli and restored my brain to normal function instantly (although my kids still doubt this sometimes!).

That was the start of a journey which lasted several years until, finally, my entire body was fully restored and healed. I spent the ensuing eight months in a wheelchair while my bones knit back together. After that, walking was very painful for a long time. As soon as I was able to stand, Gordon and I made the decision to return to work alongside Reinhard Bonnke, first in Africa and then in the Philippines. It was there, almost four years after my accident, that a couple called Charles and Frances Hunter prayed over me and God touched me powerfully as I described earlier in this book in chapter one.

God had done so much for me so, naturally, I have an immense sense of gratitude and hope in this area of healing. When you have had a near death experience and know God answered prayer, trust me, your hope is awakened and you want to pray as never before!

HOPE FOR HEALING

We read in the book of Exodus that God promises to be our God of healing.

> He said, "If you listen carefully to the voice of the LORD your God and do what is right in his eyes, if you pay attention to his commands and keep all his decrees, I will not bring on you any of the diseases I brought on the Egyptians, for I am the LORD, who heals you."
> **— EXODUS 15:26**

Right here we are given permission by God to hope for healing. It is not our idea: God asks us to expect healing. However, God wants us to be attentive to Him as we stir our expectation for health and healing in our bodies. God asks us to change our behaviour and give Him our more focused attention and obedience. He wants to heal. But, like Gideon, whose story we read in Judges, we can feel that if God is with us and wants to heal us, why is there so much sickness all around us? Let's read this scripture:

> The angel of the LORD came and sat down under the oak in Ophrah that belonged to Joash the Abiezrite, where his son Gideon was threshing wheat in a winepress to keep it from the Midianites. ¹²When the angel of the LORD appeared to Gideon, he said, "The LORD is with you, mighty warrior." ¹³"But sir," Gideon replied, "if the LORD is with us, why has all this happened to us? Where are all his wonders that our fathers told us about when they said, 'Did not the LORD bring us up out of Egypt?' But now the LORD has abandoned us and put us into the hand of Midian." ¹⁴The LORD turned to him and said, "Go in the strength you have and save Israel out of Midian's hand. Am I not sending you?" "But Lord", ¹⁵Gideon asked, "how can I save Israel? My clan is the weakest in Manasseh, and I am the least in my family."

> [16]The LORD answered, "I will be with you, and you will strike down all the Midianites together."
> — **JUDGES 6:11 ONWARDS**

What is the assurance of this hope for healing? The answer is, "the Lord is with us!" Gideon is confused by the chaos he sees all around him. He feels totally inadequate to bring any change but God appears to him and challenges him to go with the strength he has. Like Gideon, we can feel that, if God is with us, why has there been such a sense of powerlessness? What has happened to all the signs and wonders that we read about in revivals or hear about on the mission fields? How do we know our hope for healing will not be misplaced? Even after his questioning, God just asks Gideon to go as he is, and He asks us to do the same. God wants us to step out with the hope we have - and pray. We need to be God's carriers of hope for healing.

Recently, when I have been speaking at conferences, I have begun asking people if they believe we see much healing in the UK or America. Usually, their response is negative. Most acknowledge we do see healing today but usually in Africa or when on missions' trips. They do not think that we see healing in our western nations. I then ask people to identify themselves by raising their hands if they have experienced a miracle of healing in their lives, or that of a close family member, in the last 6 months. Practically everywhere forty percent of the congregation will raise their hands and sometimes this percentage has been higher! The evidence says we are seeing healing in our cities and towns in the UK and America but we are just not recognising it. God promises that He will heal us. So now let our hope and expectation for physical healing in our western nations arise. It is happening; but can we see it?

There are so many scriptures that we can use to awaken our faith and conviction. We need to read them and let them stir our vision:

> Jesus Christ the same yesterday, and today, and forever.
> — **HEBREWS 13:8**

> I tell you the truth, anyone who has faith in me will do what I have been doing. He will do even greater things than these, because I am going to the Father.
> **— JOHN 14:12**

> "I do believe; help me overcome my unbelief!"
> **— MARK 9:24**

God's heart never changes. He is the same, yesterday, today and forever. He has always wanted us to live hope filled lives, free from all pain, sickness and disease. God does not change. But now He is asking us if we will begin partnering with Him and do the work. I am not sure if we will do greater works in terms of impact but I do believe that God wants us to do greater works in terms of quantity and longevity. After all, Jesus was only on the earth for three years. God has promised us, if we will partner with Him, we will see greater works. What an opportunity! But we need to get past our unbelief and intellectual reasoning, have hope and believe that God is sending us. Remember, everything is possible for him who believes.

ACTIVATION

Take a moment and think about your body, soul and mind – is it well with your soul?

Ask God to give you hope for healing in your life.

Think about this promise – "I am the God who heals you!".

Ask God to show you where you can inspire hope for healing in others.

Write it down.

Then, like Gideon, decide to go in the strength you have and bless someone.

YES - JESUS HEALS

> He who forgives all your sins and heals all your diseases.
> — **PSALM 103:3**

I have the joy of being part of a vibrant, Jesus loving church in Oxford. I have found many great friends in our community and I always enjoy a Sunday at home in my own church. Recently, I was away preaching when I received a text from one of our ministry leaders saying that my friend, Nikki, had been rushed to hospital in severe pain straight from the Sunday service. They were asking me to pray. Once I had a moment to phone, I called Nikki's husband. He informed me that Nikki had just had a scan and that they had found a significant kidney stone lodged in a tricky part of her kidney, hence the extreme pain. I began to think of all the practical ways in which I could help when, suddenly, I found myself remembering a story my dad had often told me.

This story had happened in India when I was nine years old. I grew up in India, the daughter of missionary parents, and went to boarding school in the Nilgiri Hills, South India. Each May, when the heat was excruciating in Mumbai, my parents would come up to the Hills for some respite and have a holiday. We would usually stay in a guest house called Brooklands, among the tea gardens. It was beautiful. One afternoon, while my Dad was resting, I was playing outside our room by the trees, when I heard my Dad screaming. I ran to our room to find my Mum trying to help Dad get to the bathroom. Mum explained he had a kidney stone. I am told I burst into the room and immediately asked to pray for my Dad. Laying hands on his lower back I asked God to take the pain away and heal him. Instantly my Dad felt relief, and over the next few days the disintegrated stone passed, and he fully recovered.

As I remembered this story, hope arose in my heart and I decided to pray for my friend, Nikki. I prayed for the total removal of this stone and any after effects and recorded a message for Nikki on WhatsApp. My hope was stirred and I trusted for healing. The next day Nikki was called by the consultant to return to the unit for further tests and treatment. After a little while, they called her back into the consulting room perplexed. They could find no trace of the stone. They had the scan taken yesterday and today's scan on the screen in front of them. One showed a significant stone, the recent scan showed nothing. It had completely gone! YES - Jesus heals today in the UK!

THE COMPLETE MAKEOVER

He who forgives all your sins and heals all your diseases.
— **PSALM 103:3**

Hope affects every part of your being – body, mind, soul, emotions. Hope requires a total rewiring of the way you approach life. When we let the hope of God fill us, it shifts every perspective of ourselves, aligns our thinking and emotions with God's worldview, and gives us a purpose and destiny for life. We begin to think as God thinks about our life and those around us. Not only does He forgive our sins but He heals our bodies and souls. God has the power to heal us from the inside out. So often it is not just the sickness of our bodies that causes us suffering but the pain in our heart that needs healing too. We need healing from the bitter memories of betrayal and times of injustice. We need freedom from the burden of regret. We need passion and purpose in life that break the monotony and sense of futility when we think about tomorrow. We need hope, healing and life! God is able to restore all these areas with hope and heal our sense of wellbeing. As the Psalmist confirms, the Good Shepherd can touch our soul:

> He restores my soul.
>
> **— PSALM 23:3**

The restoration of your soul requires a different kind of atmosphere to the healing of your body. For your soul to be restored, it needs to be in a quiet and safe place where you can trust God to walk with you through painful memories and bring hope. A broken heart cannot be mended by a medical doctor but God can restore it. This process often takes time and needs kindness and gentleness.

JESUS DELIVERS

Jesus comes to deliver us from the torment of the mind. In the Bible we read about demons and evil spirits but these words can legitimately be translated as tormenting spirits too. Sometimes this translation can help us have a better perspective of the deliverance we need and can receive. So many people living around us are tormented by addictions to alcohol, drugs, pornography or gambling, and people find themselves trapped. Others are gripped by phobias, fears and anxieties and feel suffocated. They are crying out for freedom and Jesus is the giver of hope in their dark world. Evil spirits are tormenting spirits and they rob people of the power to think clearly and accept the truth about who they are. In Jesus we have hope for total healing. We read this wonderful story of hope and freedom in Luke:

> Then people went out to see what had happened, and they came to Jesus and found the man from whom the demons had gone, sitting at the feet of Jesus, clothed and in his right mind, and they were afraid. [36]And those who had seen it told them how the demon-possessed man had been healed. [37]Then all the people of the surrounding country of the Gerasenes asked him to depart from them, for they were seized with great fear.

So he got into the boat and returned. [38]The man from whom the demons had gone begged that he might be with him, but Jesus sent him away, saying, [39]"Return to your home, and declare how much God has done for you." And he went away, proclaiming throughout the whole city how much Jesus had done for him.
— **LUKE 8:35-39**

We can have hope for radical, total healing in Jesus. People who have lived in fear and terror are able to break free and sit at the feet of Jesus and be made whole. Their mind is restored and they can think again. They can sleep again. Jesus wants to release us from the terror of our minds. He brings hope and we can truly say – "Wow, it is well with my soul!"

STORY FROM BETEL

I have had the wonderful privilege of ministering to, and getting to know, many people who have been part of the Betel family and who have journeyed from the hopelessness of addictions and found hope. They have found Jesus, freedom and a new life. They now live a hope filled life, delivered from their past, and totally restored. Here is the testimony of Kelly (Gibson) Williams, a treasure found in Watford. Please read this extract from Betel's book Escaping Addictions. This is a story of deliverance and hope:

> *"I was a mess. I had no one to turn to for help. I was wild, so I began the cycle of running away, new man, new baby, drugs, alcohol, and violence - repeat."*

> *Kelly grew up with an alcoholic mum who experienced a lot of violence from the men in her life. Unfortunately Kelly and her younger brother were exposed to it as well. At seven or eight years old, on a bus coming home from a fun outing with her mum and her boyfriend, Kelly and her brother witnessed*

a gruesome scene in which the boyfriend beat their mum unrecognisable because she refused to cuddle Kelly. At ten years old she yet again witnessed another terrible rape and beating of her mum by this man. The next morning Kelly called a crisis hotline and they were taken to a safe house and never saw that man again.

Things went from bad to worse. Kelly and her brother were taken from a situation where they were witnessing violence to a new situation where they were the victims of violence. They were taken to a children's care home where Kelly, at the age of 9 years old, was sexually abused by a 14 year old girl. "I was crying out for comfort, love and attention. This just confused me, it didn't feel right. I would wet the bed till I was 12 and I couldn't sleep in the dark until recently, at 35 years old. I was terrified and full of fear."

At 15 Kelly started taking cocaine and by 16 she was taking all types of drugs, pills, speed, and smoking heroin. Since both of her parents were addicts it was easy to score and use at any time. At 17 she had her first of five children. "I felt so empty, so numb. I just wanted to feel loved, wanted and normal."

Life became even more unbearable the day she found out her brother, who was everything to her, went missing. "I lost control, I wanted to die. I would lay in my bed hoping to die in my sleep. I would get so wrecked, I wouldn't care if I lost all dignity."

Sitting on a dirty mattress full of burn marks, completely incoherent, Kelly was suddenly awakened with an immediacy. She pushed open her door to see her two year old daughter, Sienna, standing in the hall flinging around a doll that was on fire. "I grabbed the doll and chucked it, at the same time throwing Sienna across the hall." Kelly kicked her daughter's door in to see the whole bed was alight. "I grabbed her and I think I must have stood there, I couldn't even tell you how long". She walked over to the father of her daughter and said, "I don't even like you. I don't know why I'm here!" She took her daughter and went to her mum's home. Standing in the bathroom at her mum's, without warning, she felt a total peace. From that moment on she never smoked heroin again.

Years later a shaft of light entered Kelly's life in the form of Nadya who was from a local church. She brought three bags of groceries and never stopped coming for two years. Kelly saw the steady, loving kindness and it caused her to ponder if there was more to life than the way she had been living. "I didn't want to live this selfish, cold, dirty lifestyle anymore; I wanted change."

It was through the patient help and prayers of Nadya that Kelly found the help she desperately needed in the form of Betel. When she walked through the doors she felt the same peace she had felt in her mum's bathroom years before- it felt familiar, yet strange. "I had a sense of belonging, I couldn't understand but I felt peace."

After nineteen months in a place of peace Kelly said, "I was free and at peace with my past. The biggest battle I faced was forgiveness: God was by my side and we faced it together, in His perfect timing, I overcame. He delivered me and I began to forgive everyone who hurt me but ultimately myself. I'm so grateful for this opportunity; no more running for me. The only place I run to is straight into God's big beautiful hands! I am safe, loved and I matter."

Talking with Kelly flushes you with excitement and passion. There is no doubt this woman can change the world. Her enthusiasm for life is truly contagious and makes you want to do something with your own life! To hear of the extreme pain and sorrow in her past life, then catch her new passion for life, is nothing short of a miracle. "I am no longer afraid of the darkness. I am now walking in the light. I am a child of God, all I did was believe! I thank God for creating me and keeping me. When I felt no worth, He was truth for me, guiding my footsteps and protecting my heart; even though I was broken, He healed me. There is beauty in my brokenness. God gets all the glory forever and ever and ever."

When asked of her dreams going forward she said, "My dream used to be that I just wanted to be happy and I have that now. Looking forward, I just want to help." Kelly has a deep compassion for people who are living like she used to. To help mums and their children find hope is something she can see herself doing in the future. She wants to be a light in the darkness to say, "You don't have to live like that anymore."

"I'll never be that person again. I'm brand new! Whatever has happened - it's over, old. It doesn't even matter now. I can just be me!"

So here we read a story of the kindness of God to find us in the midst of our pain and deliver us from torment. God can change the narrative of our life. He brings us good news. As we are healed, He then sends us out to carry this message to others. Out of our mess, God creates a message of hope.

LAY YOUR HANDS, GOD WILL BRING RECOVERY

[7]As you go, preach this message: 'The kingdom of heaven is near.' [8]Heal the sick, raise the dead, cleanse those who have leprosy, drive out demons.

— **MATTHEW 10:7-8**

We now have the honour to carry this message of hope and bring the atmosphere of heaven near to people in their everyday lives. We carry this message – the Kingdom of Heaven is close to you right now. He is a God who can heal the sick, drive out torment and cleanse your conscience.

> [17]And these signs will accompany those who believe: In my name they will drive out demons, [18]they will speak in new tongues; they will lay their hands on the sick and they will recover.
> — **MARK 16:17-18**

When we worked with Reinhard Bonnke in Africa, I remember how he instructed us to pray for the sick. In his gruff, passionate voice he inspired us to pray for anyone. "After all, you never know unless you have a go!", he stated. "Just find a sick person, lay your hands appropriately on their body, and pray for them to be healed. Your job is to lay your hands on a sick person and God's job is to bring the recovery." Once I asked Reinhard what we should do when nothing happens? How should we pray then? He responded, "Just pray again as if everyone has been healed. Keep praying. Remember Rachel," he challenged me, "No one will ever die because you simply prayed for them, but someone may die because you chose not to pray." Keep praying for everyone, everywhere, even when you feel nothing is happening. God wants to heal, and He wants to use you!

In the first book of John we read:

> The reason the Son of God appeared was to destroy the devil's work.
> — **1 JOHN 3:8**

Here we read that Jesus came to earth to seek and save the lost. He came as a saviour, healer and deliverer. On the cross Jesus took all my sin and, through the beating and the stripes on His back, He also took all my sickness and disease. Then He wore a crown of thorns and bore all my mental torment and emotional anguish. Jesus took it all. He opened the door of hope and made a way for me to live a hope filled life. There is hope for healing and the total restoration of our lives. God will heal you.

ACTIVATION

Just take a moment to thank Jesus, the one who saves, heals and delivers.

Write down some of your memories of those times when God touched your life.

Do you know the hope of this freedom in your life? Pray and thank Him.

Ask God for a new confidence to lay your hands on the sick and pray.

What stories of healing do you know about? Write them down.

5

HOPE FILLED

When hope has seemed hopeless

"And in the end, it is not the years in your life that count. It is the LIFE in your years!"
— **ABRAHAM LINCOLN**

HOPE AGAINST HOPE

Against all hope, Abraham in hope believed and so became the father of many nations, just as it had been said to him, "so shall your offspring be." [19]Without weakening in his faith, he faced the fact that his body was a good as dead - since he was about 100 years old - and that Sarah's womb was also dead. [20]Yet he did not waver through unbelief regarding the promise of God, but was strengthened in his faith and gave glory to God, [21]being fully persuaded that God had power to do what He had promised.
— **ROMANS 4:18-21**

We have looked at the promises of healing, read the miraculous testimonies, and we can feel our hope rise. God is a healer. Yet our experiences in this area of healing can be the greatest challenges to our hope. As we read this scripture about Abraham, we realise that he, too, had to endure a struggle with his hope and faith.

He hoped against all hope! Many of us can immediately recognise this wrestle. So how do we hold fast to our hope and let God persuade us that He is still with us when everything turns sour? The apparent facts and our hope in God seem to contradict each other, so what should we believe? This is the battle of hope against hope!

EXPLORING THE COMPLEXITY OF HOPE

How do we handle hopelessness when God does not heal our disease? What then? How do we remain hope filled when our heart is suffering and our desire to see physical healing for a friend has not been realised? Unfortunately, we will probably all face these dilemmas in the course of our lives. As the quote by Abraham Lincoln above challenges us, should we be fighting for longevity of life or quality of life lived? When we feel confused by a life lost in the early years, is there another perspective of hope? All of us have to learn to navigate these twin tracks of life, both the sweet and the sour seasons with God. Hope and despair. Ease and difficulty. Euphoria and disappointments. Celebrations and pain. Goodness and suffering. This is part of life. All life's random happenings tend to trigger these conflicting emotions. A broken marriage – a failed exam – a rejected job offer – a life threatening disease – the death of a friend or partner – the betrayal of trust…and so many more life experiences that all collide with our hope and can leave us overwhelmed. But, at the same time, we will hear news that there has been a baby born against all the odds – a life spared – a marriage healed – a promotion beyond expectation – a generous gift of kindness… and many other hope filled stories that bring immense joy. We live with the continuous tension of hopes fulfilled, followed by days of despair when hope is lost.

So how do we maintain our hope in God consistently in the midst of these experiences? This is the very essence of the complexity of this struggle for hope. The sweet and sour – the ecstasy and the pain – the highs and the lows. Even as I write this book, I am walking this path in a very personal and real way myself. Most of you who read this book will not have known Anna Farley, our co-pastor with Craig here in our church in Oxford. On 30 March 2023, Anna unexpectedly died, graduated to Heaven and went to be with Jesus. Against all our hopes, she died even though we had believed for a miracle. We prayed, we hoped, we were sure she would be healed, but now we have to process the grief, the loss, and the disappointment that she is gone. Walking through these deep seasons of the soul is difficult but essential. The Bible expresses it this way, saying that we need to recognise the time and season for many different emotions of our hearts. We read this in the book of Ecclesiastes:

> ¹There is a time for everything, and a season for every activity under the heavens: ²a time to be born and a time to die, a time to plant and a time to uproot, ³a time to kill and a time to heal, a time to tear down and a time to build, ⁴a time to weep and a time to laugh, a time to mourn and a time to dance.
> — **ECCLESIASTES 3:1-4**

Even in the midst of our tears, we still need to keep a healthy perspective of every other season of life too. We should still be ready to celebrate good news as we process our loss. Here in the midst of being overwhelmed by our disappointed hope, we must still see there is good news too! We weep with those who weep and still are able to rejoice with those who rejoice. We can never allow ourselves to become hopeless.

HANDLING PAIN BECAUSE WE HOPED

But did we get it wrong? Should we have prayed for healing only to feel so disappointed now? Were we wrong to hope? I always think of the story of King David in the Bible when I am grappling with these thoughts. Let us read the story in the second book of Samuel:

> [18]On the seventh day the child died. David's attendants were afraid to tell him that the child was dead, for they thought, "While the child was still living, he wouldn't listen to us when we spoke to him. How can we now tell him the child is dead? He may do something desperate." [19]David noticed that his attendants were whispering among themselves, and he realised the child was dead. "Is the child dead?", he asked. "Yes," they replied, "he is dead." [20]Then David got up from the ground. After he had washed, put on lotions and changed his clothes, he went into the house of the Lord and worshipped. Then he went to his own house, and at his request they served him food, and he ate. [21]His attendants asked him, "Why are you acting this way? While the child was alive, you fasted and wept, but now that the child is dead, you get up and eat!" [22]He answered, "While the child was still alive, I fasted and wept. I thought, 'Who knows? The Lord may be gracious to me and let the child live.' [23]But now that he is dead, why should I go on fasting? Can I bring him back again?"
>
> **— 2 SAMUEL 12:18-23**

King David had prayed hard, fasted and cried out to God. But his baby had died. Once he knew God had taken his child, he stopped praying and worshipped. He knew he had finished what he could do. So he got up, released his responsibility to pray for his son, and worshipped God instead. Those around him were confused. But David does not give us any apology for praying for a miracle right up until the last moment. He was totally focused in prayer. When David was asked about his attitude, he replied that he had prayed until he was certain about God's decision but, once the child had died, he knew he was released. His child had gone, God had made His decision.

I, too, have made a risky choice. I have decided that I would rather knock on the door of Heaven passionately and pray for healing and a miracle, even if I risk the pain of disappointment, than not pray at all. Usually, the sick person will ask you to take a stand and pray with them. The family will also want you to pray and the church should also pray so how can we possibly say we have decided not to pray for healing? I do not understand why these prayer battles are not always answered with a healing story. I hate the feeling of hope deferred, and the pain of loss, but I still cannot find it in my heart not to pray for a miracle. I am alive today because courageous people prayed, fasted and fought for my life. God heard their cry and I am forever grateful that people were courageous enough to pray for my life. We have to risk again and pray for healing. In moments of loss, we can feel a complex mix of emotions but, even so, we must continue to pray for miraculous healing. We should know that praying time is never wasted time, even when we cannot guarantee the outcome. The church is called to pray for the sick.

Earlier I shared my story about praying for Nikki and her kidney stone. I was feeling very raw emotionally when I prayed for her healing as I was still processing the loss of Anna. But when I heard of the pain she was experiencing and remembered how God had healed my Dad's kidney stone, my hope had stirred. I felt God ask me, "Rachel, are you going to keep your hands in your pocket from now on? Do you not believe in the prayer of healing? Have you lost your hope?" I felt challenged to take my hands and pray once again and God heard this cry. Nikki was healed from the kidney stone and delivered from pain. Even though it is not always easy, I believe we cannot hide our hands in our pockets – we must pray and watch God do miracles.

FINDING OUR HOPE AGAIN AFTER LOSS

1. DECIDE TO TRUST GOD, REGARDLESS OF THE CIRCUMSTANCES

When you have prayed for change and nothing happens, or it gets even worse; when you have believed for healing and the person dies rather than be healed; when you have asked for a family and you still have no child; when your job situation is stagnant, and your finances are pressed and you have given faithfully to God but there is no answer; how do you still maintain your trust in God? You have to make stubborn resolutions to believe God and His word and not your circumstances. We cannot let our circumstances define the face of God and His goodness in our lives.

We hear the cry of Job – "Yet though you slay me, I will trust you!" But what does this verse from Job 13:15 mean practically in our world today? Well, it sounds like this: "God, we believe in you. We trust in you and we know that, in you, we always have hope. So, no matter what we're walking through, no matter what we're facing, our hope must be rooted in you. Our hope is not in anyone or anything else. Even though I do not understand these circumstances, and I do not like them, I know that I love you, God, even more and so, somehow, I will trust you!" This feeling of being slain, cut to the core, that Job expresses is very real in these deep moments. We can really feel as though God is killing us! But do not allow yourself to get offended with God. Remind yourself that God is good - all the time. But sometimes it just does not feel like it! Make a courageous decision to trust God Himself, and not your circumstances, and take lots of time to worship.

2. FIND COURAGE TO KEEP TALKING TO GOD

> "O LORD Almighty, God of Israel, you have revealed this to your servant, saying, 'I will build a house for you.' So your servant has found courage to offer you this prayer. O Sovereign LORD, you are God! Your words are trustworthy, and you have promised these good things to your servant."
> **— 2 SAMUEL 7:27**

It takes courage to keep talking to God when your life is not making sense. Here David knows he has been called by God for a purpose but He cannot see the way forward. However, he still finds courage to keep having a conversation with God about it. Too often, when life becomes difficult, we withdraw from God and stop talking to Him. Even if these are difficult conversations, have the courage to keep talking to God, expressing your heart, and listening to Him. We need to respond like David and find courage, continuing to pray, keeping our hearts tender with praise, and declaring that His word is trustworthy. In Hebrews, Paul explains why it is so important to hold fast to your hope and faith in tough times. Let us read this passage:

> [35]So do not throw away your confidence; it will be richly rewarded. [36]You need to persevere so that when you have done the will

> of God, you will receive what he has promised. [37]For in just a very little while, "He who is coming will come and will not delay. [38]But my righteous one will live by faith. And if he shrinks back, I will not be pleased with him." [39]But we are not of those who shrink back and are destroyed, but of those who believe and are saved. [1]Now faith is being sure of what we hope for and certain of what we do not see.
> **— HEBREWS 10:35-11:1**

It takes great courage to keep doing what is right, especially when our circumstances do not make sense any longer. We need to be filled with fresh hope, by the Holy Spirit. God is in control and He does care and has a perfect plan, even when life is tough and everything seems impossible. We must not throw away our confidence in God.

3. GOD IS STILL GOD

Your circumstances may have changed drastically but God is still the same God, so do not lose sight of Him. Do not let your circumstances cause you to change your view of God. Keep hold of your understanding of His nature. Remember He is the same God who still loves you passionately and cares about every detail of your life. God is still God and He never changes.

> Jesus Christ is the same yesterday and today and forever.
> **— HEBREWS 13:8**

Many years ago now, I remember meeting a little boy who had just lost his dad in a tragic road accident in Kenya. His dad had been a youth pastor and worship leader; I was visiting the church and knew his wife and wanted to comfort her. However, what I remember most about that day was my extraordinary conversation with Daniel. He opened the conversation by saying that he did not feel that Jesus was very kind. When I asked him why, he explained to me that he thought Jesus ought to share his daddy with him. I waited for a fuller explanation and he said, "Well, I have talked with mummy and she says that Jesus wants my daddy to live with Him in Heaven in his house now. But I want daddy to come to my house and live with me too. So I have asked mummy if Jesus can share. I would like daddy to come and live with me in my house in the holidays and then my daddy can go and live with Jesus sometimes too. But mummy says that Jesus cannot do this, and daddy has to stay in his house in Heaven. So, I do not think that Jesus is very kind because Jesus should know how to share!" This explanation made a lot of sense, especially if you were about seven years old.

While I was still thinking about this conversation, Daniel suddenly jumped up and went to find his toy guitar. He often used to stand behind his dad pretending to play, while his dad led the worship in church. "What song are you going to play, Daniel?", I asked. "Oh, my favourite, He is still God." He then began to sing a song that Godfrey Birtill had written about the different challenging situations we can find ourselves in and how we still have to say – "He is still God". "When we're desperate for our healing, still God, still God, still God. You're still God". Daniel knew the lyrics perfectly. But as I continued to listen to him sing, I suddenly realised that he had changed the words. He had now added his own version. "When you take my daddy to Heaven, You are still God, still God, still God…". What a statement from the sincere heart of a little boy! He could not understand much but he still understood enough to say, "even though I don't like this – you are still God."

So whatever the circumstances that are challenging your hope, remember to sing "He is still God" and acknowledge that He does not change.

4. ASK THE INTELLIGENT QUESTIONS

> ¹As he went along, he saw a man blind from birth. ²His disciples asked him, "Rabbi, who sinned, this man or his parents, that he was born blind?" ³"Neither this man nor his parents sinned," said Jesus, "but this happened so that the works of God might be displayed in him."
> — **JOHN 9:1-3**

The disciples wanted to know why this man was blind. They were trying to find a simplistic reason to explain to themselves why this man was in this condition. They were asking the "why" question. But Jesus does not answer their question of why; instead, he tells them that a better perspective would be to ask yourself, "what is the opportunity in this situation?". In our rational approach to life, we often try to process an answer to life's questions in the wrong way. There are times when we should not ask this "why" question. We need to recognise that asking the wrong question in times of struggle can open up a dialogue of doubt and questioning that becomes unhelpful. Jesus advises us that the more intelligent question is to ask Him, "what is the purpose of this difficulty in my life? What will happen as a result of this season?". We need to ask the questions that look to the future, not our past!

As you watch people's journey of life around you, you soon realise that bad things do happen to very good people. Conversely, good things also happen to bad people, which is very annoying! So we cannot have cliché answers as to the reason people suffer. Life does not always have simple answers. God lost His own son at 30 years old. Jesus died young, without ever getting married or having a family. He was persecuted, tormented and murdered. We, too, are called to be soldiers for Christ and this has a price. Unjust and unrighteous events will touch our lives too. There are many times when we will know divine protection and escape. But there will also be times when we have to make a sacrifice. We may have to walk through the fire and the floods but we need to know they will not overwhelm us even though we may get hot and wet in the process!

5. REMEMBER THE END IS NOT THE END UNTIL IT IS THE END

When a friend dies of cancer, you can be tempted to think, "this is the end". But even physical death is not the final end of the story in the economy of God. There is hope beyond hope. Paul speaks about this hope that is eternal. We never need to be hopeless, even in death. We have to see our eternal hope against all other hopes. I believe Heaven is an upgrade, not a downgrade. The person who knows Jesus can never lose their life or their hope. Their hope remains. As Paul writes in 1 Corinthians 15:55: "Where, O death, is your victory? Where, O death, is your sting?" Death has lost its grip on us. This is especially true for the person battling illness and hoping for healing. Even if they do die, they die hope filled. Jesus carried all our disease and suffering, and He dealt with every sickness including every unusual, rare disease, He went to the cross for it all. Now it is His battle and not ours. We can have full hope because we know the end of the story and He WON! The challenge we have is this: we cannot guarantee on which side of eternity we will see or experience this victory in our bodies - but we will see the hope of our healing fulfilled. The end is not the end until God says it is the end. God has placed eternity in our hearts. Eternity is hard-wired within each of us by design. We always want to live forever and, because of Jesus, we can. Time here together may never feel "enough". We always want to live on earth forever; we want so much more, here and now. But when we surrender our lives to God, we also surrender the right to our life and we let Him direct us. He has marked out the exact number of the days of our life, whether here on earth or in Heaven. So we choose to trust him.

Our hope remains intact, whether lived on earth or in Heaven. There is a greater story unfolding and we can hope in this.

ACTIVATION

We have discussed 5 steps that help us hold onto our hope in times of loss.

Remind yourself of each step.

1. Decide to trust. 2. Find courage to pray 3. He is still God 4. Ask the intelligent questions. 5. The end is not the end until God says so!

Write down the action points you need to consider. How has God spoken to you?

Now stop and take a moment to consider Heaven. What is our eternal hope – the hope beyond hope?

HEAVENLY HOPE

For us left behind, we still experience the sting of separation after someone's death and the loss of their friendship. Our earthly hopes and dreams are shaken so we need to glimpse into the hope of Heaven. How do we bear this sting of grief and lost hope? We have to ask God to show us His bigger hope filled picture beyond our loss. We have to see Heaven and understand this world beyond our world. We learn to experience God's goodness in different ways, not always in the ways we had hoped for, but often in surprising ways. We have to learn to hope beyond hope.

We need to understand that as Christians we live in two different time zones at the same time. Our spiritual nature lives in Heaven's time, "kairos". This time is connected to eternity; it is cyclical time where the end and the beginning of time are held together in the same moment. God knows the end from the beginning. But as humans we also live in "chronos" time. This is the chronological, linear timescale. We live with a concept of a yesterday, today and a future that unfolds in a timeline. Here is the clash of understandings. Here is where we hope against hope and we have to recognise that God has a plan beyond our earthly hopes and dreams. God knows how to work all these things for good – if we can still love and trust Him. The end is never the end until God says it is the end. There is hope beyond hope. Let us read this scripture:

> I make known the end from the beginning, from ancient times, what is still to come. I say: My purpose will stand, and I will do all that I please.
> — **ISAIAH 46:10**

Here we are reminded of the eternal plan of God. Even death does not destroy or alter the plans of God for our lives: even after His death, Jesus had fulfilled His divine purpose. Death cannot ruin God's plan. The end is not the end but it may alter the hopes and dreams we held and the way we thought we would accomplish them. But remember that, however confusing the challenge of your hopes may be right now, God has a plan and He is able to fulfil it. Your hope can live again.

THE MIRACLE OF HOPE

Let us finish this chapter with a story of hope and remind ourselves of the goodness of God.

Dear Rachel.

You don't know me, but I want to share an answered prayer. My name is Elisabeth. I am married to a pastor and we now have two beautiful children. I had almost lost hope that it would ever be possible to have this second baby. I had preeclampsia, and the birth of my daughter was difficult. My daughter was premature and only weighed 1400g at birth but we wanted to have one more child. I was at a women's conference in Grimstad in February 2016, Norway. Friday night you said that God has spoken to you about a woman who had just experienced a bleed and had lost their baby in a miscarriage. I started to cry, as it spoke to my heart, but I thought there must be many women who could have experienced the same. So I did not respond. Again on Saturday night you said that God wanted to minister to a woman who had just miscarried, and you came and walked over to me and prayed for me even though you didn't know who I was.

Then later, while you were preaching on this same Saturday night, you suddenly spoke to me and said that you saw the Holy Spirit all over me, resting on me, and so I came to the front and you prayed for me. It was fantastic, and I cried, and I was so comforted that God saw me. You see this is my story. I had just come home from the hospital after my third spontaneous miscarriage. This third time was very dramatic with the pregnancy growing outside the womb. The doctors had had to take away one of my fallopian tubes, so I only have one left. I also was kept in hospital for one week as I contracted an infection in the surgery wounds. I came to the meeting having almost lost hope that I would ever have a successful pregnancy and a second child.

After that night I went home to my husband and we prayed a lot. I was so encouraged that God saw me, and that he gave me hope. I became pregnant again and I am so thankful that it went so well. My healthy son was born in January 2017, it was a natural birth and we could have him in our room the first night we got him. Hallelujah.

I just want to thank you that God saw me when I had no hope. We are so grateful for our son, Johannes!!!!

God bless you!
— Elisabeth

ACTIVATION

Sit in the presence of God and let hope arise.

Remember He is the God who sees you. He knows you and has an answer for you.

Write down what He says to you.

6

HOPE FILLED

For our financial future

> "God gave me my money. I believe the power to make money is a gift from God. It should be developed and used to the best of our ability for the good of mankind. Having been endowed with the gift I possess, I believe it is my duty to make money and still more money and to use the money I make for the good of my fellow man according to the dictates of my conscience."
> — **JOHN D ROCKEFELLER (1839-1937),**
> *American industrialist and philanthropist*

Nothing can open a door to a foreboding sense of hopelessness like the news of financial ruin. Very quickly successful people who have been made redundant can find themselves struggling with depression. Somehow, within the depths of our being, God created us with the need to work, produce and provide and, when we can't do this, we quickly find ourselves battling with worthlessness. We lose our will to live. Many successful company directors, high flying entrepreneurs and creative thinkers, carry a strong sense of hope but, if they lose their money, roles or job they crash into despair. This quote by John Rockefeller is a good reminder of the purpose of wealth and the hope we should carry when stewarding our money for God.

Most media headlines around us in this season seem to be predicting our financial disaster. We are surrounded by stories that sap our hope. We are constantly being told that we will not be able to pay our utility bills as they sky rocket and so our families will freeze this winter. Our pension funds will disappear and so there will not be enough to support us in our old age. Our wages are decreasing and will not cover the food bills. We are bombarded with threatening stories of our financial ruin. It takes stubborn resilience to trust God with your financial future when you are living in the midst of these continuous negative financial forecasts. So how do we keep anchored in hope and keep sane? Do we know what foundation our financial security is based upon? What are the promises of God that we must understand to access His financial supply in these seasons of financial turbulence? In God we can find hope for a secure financial future.

THE MOST GENEROUS PERSON I KNOW

God is the most generous giver of all. He will never fail me. My security in the midst of financial turmoil is rooted in this discovery. I have come to know His character, experienced His supply and trust it implicitly, and I know He will provide. This is where my hope is grounded. Whenever I encounter times of financial challenge, I know in the very depth of my being that my God will provide for me. Since He has proven it over the years, I am now confident of this hope when it comes to financial issues. Let's take some time to discover this amazing Provider for ourselves.

We can often have the mentality that our employer is our provider since he pays our wages. But we need to realise that our financial security should be founded on God, not the company. God is the source of our resources. It is He who showers us with good gifts, not the company!

Let's read some scriptures together to discover the source of our financial hope:

> Every good gift and every perfect gift is from above, coming down from the Father of lights with whom there is no variation or shadow due to change.
> **— JAMES 1:17 (ESV)**

Remember every gift of provision comes from above. It comes down from your Father in Heaven. In His Kingdom there is no time of recession or lack, no times of financial change. He is a consistent supplier. God is the giver of perfect gifts.

> For you know the grace of our Lord Jesus Christ, that though he was rich, yet for your sake he became poor, so that you by his poverty might become rich.
> **— 2 CORINTHIANS 8:9 (ESV)**

We also need to understand that God gave to us when we had nothing to give back. He gave out of His riches, when we were in our poverty. He did not give expecting anything in return. God gave to us generously, knowing we could never repay Him. This was not manipulative giving - but a generous gift.

> For God so loved the world, that he gave his only Son, that whoever believes in him should not perish but have eternal life.
> **— JOHN 3:16 (ESV)**

God also gave us of the very best that He had. He did not give us a second-class gift. He gave us the best and it was a very sacrificial gift. This gift cost Him everything. God, our Father, is the most generous giver of ALL! This is a God we can trust in times of trouble. We can put our hope in Him.

GOD'S PERFECT SOLUTION

Here is a testimony of God's perfect provision when we decide to let Him be the provider.

Hallelujah, just a quick testimony. This time I allowed Jesus, the Lion of the tribe of Judah, to fight for me and not the tiger I find within myself! The money I was owed for a job I did for a company since last February, nearly 9 months ago now, has been paid in full. Hallelujah. There was a difficult situation around this job, but I have been believing God to get my money out for me. But the constant delay was frustrating me. I was planning to send an angry email to the owner of the company, but God asked me to stay still, and your word on Saturday was a confirmation. So today, God led me to send a very nice text, not an email, to the CEO. She usually doesn't reply to any text or even email. In fact I always have to send her any message via her PA but today she replied to my text immediately. She apologised for the delay, asked me to resend my invoice and then paid it instantly. I praise God – He has answered my cry.

— A.I.

HOPE FILLED GENEROSITY

> [12]Wealth and honour come from you; you are the ruler of all things. In your hands are strength and power to exalt and give strength to all. [13]Now, our God, we give you thanks, and praise your glorious name. [14]"But who am I, and who are my people, that we should be able to give as generously as this? Everything comes from you, and we have given you only what comes from your hand.
> — **1 CHRONICLES 29:12-14**

Here we see David has the revelation that, even when we think we are being generous, we are only able to give because God has already given to us. God is the source of all giving. He is the God of all generosity. Firstly, He has given to us and now He gives us the privilege to partner with Him and become givers too. This is where our confidence in financial situations should be rooted. Often we can hesitate when we feel God ask us to give a gift, worrying that we will deplete our resources by giving this gift. But we need to understand that God is the giver of everything and we just have the privilege to be part of His divine cycle of generosity. God is well able to meet our every need. We need to allow this confident hope to grow in our lives.

> And my God will meet all your needs according to the riches of his glory in Christ Jesus.
> — **PHILIPPIANS 4:19**

This is such a well-known scripture. It is probably the one where our hope for God's provision is based. However, there is often a great deal of discussion about what the definition of this word "need" means. If you are from a more conservative church background, you will be told – "God will provide your needs, but not all your wants!" Somehow caught up in this statement is the advice that you should only expect to receive the bare minimum from God. We should not be greedy. I remember growing up in my missionary boarding school and being trained to think like this. However, I believe that God loves to be generous towards us although He does not satisfy the desires of a greedy or covetous heart. He recognises a pure heart that loves Jesus and will lavishly provide.

About ten years ago, my mother wanted to go to Australia to visit her relatives, see her grandchildren and also just walk the land. It was also going to be her 80th birthday, her 60th wedding anniversary and 50 years in the ministry, all within a couple of months. This was a time for celebration. My Dad was not capable of making such a trip at this time, so I offered to take her and travel with her. I really wanted to bless her but financially we were stretched and I was not sure what resources we had available to do this. Then my mind began to wonder, would God provide for this type of trip? Was this a true need or more like lavish greed? Could I ask God to supply these tickets? Pushing aside these conflicting thoughts, I prayed, honestly asking God to give us the finances so that I could take Mum and bless her. The next day, nearly immediately, God provided $15,000 to pay for both airfares, specifying that the tickets should be bought in business class. God, it seemed, was very happy to provide, even giving us both an upgrade! What a generous God. Put your hope in the bank account of God!

You may be reading this story and feel that God never provides for you like that. But I have discovered that, when we pray and ask God to help us, we can then sometimes miss the way He does provide. The supply is not always as simple as cash in the bank. We are often blind to creative ways in which we do receive the provision of God. Do you recognise the bargain in the shop when an item you wanted is now on sale; or the tax refund which came so unexpectedly and paid a bill; or a coupon or voucher that doubled your spending power? You ask God for a holiday and suddenly your parents offer to take you away with them, all expenses paid. You need a new car and an older aunt offers you hers, as she no longer wants to drive. You need some new clothes for the children and a friend gifts you with boxes of clothes from her children of the same age that they no longer use, all in great condition. Are you able to recognise the many sources God uses to provide? Unexpected bonuses, a discounted bargain, free tickets for a film you wanted to see, a refund that you did not expect….and so the list goes on. Learn to recognise the provision of God and be grateful. He does not fail.

LESSONS OF HOPE & FINANCE

"Having, first, gained all you can, and then secondly saved all you can, then give all you can. When I have money, I get rid of it quickly, lest it find a way into my heart for it is much easier to save a man's soul than his pocket."
— **JOHN WESLEY**

Nothing tests your heart like money! The wrestling of your hope during times of financial lack tests your simple trust in the care of God. Do you believe that God is a good provider? Does He care for you? Like the faith challenges in the areas of health discussed earlier, financial hardship also confronts the basis of our hope and confidence in God.

Psychologists say that we have three basic, instinctive needs that have to be met in order to establish a healthy relationship. They have identified these as a sense of security, self-worth and significance. When you find yourself in a season of financial hardship, all three of these foundational stones are tested. We can feel a failure and worthless when we are unable to provide: we lose our sense of self-worth and value. We are overwhelmed with anxiety and fears as we may lose our home and possessions: we feel insecure and unsafe. We are confused about our future and the way forward and can only see disaster ahead: we lose our purpose and significance. For our hope to survive these times of economic challenge, we must keep our minds rooted on God's word, keep listening to what God says about our life, and remain secure and connected in our relationship with Him. Your hope will be shaken and stirred but you must look to God and keep standing firm. Not always easy but necessary! So let us take a moment and reflect and let God help us.

ACTIVATION

How is your hope in God concerning your finances?

Are you secure with God – do you trust Him to provide?

Do you feel you are a worthy investment and valuable to God?

Do you know your significant purpose or is it tied up with your role and work?

Ask God to show you how He loves to provide for you. Write it down and thank Him.

Play some worship music and let God speak to you about His funds and assets.

GOD WILL PROVIDE

Our house in Oxford has a name plate, just to the left of our gate, as you enter our property. Gordon lovingly carved this wooden sign many years ago with the name "MORIAH" as a sign of hope when we had no hope. We were desperately trusting God to give us a home in the UK on our return from living as missionaries in Africa.

At the time it seemed impossible that we would ever own a house where we could hang this name plaque. We had little prospect of being able to buy a place for our family after eight years of being away on the mission field. The markets had changed, everything was so expensive, our cash reserves had depleted, and we had no option of a mortgage as we had not been resident in the UK long enough to qualify. We prayed and hoped against hope. Then we got a home! God did provide in miraculous ways and we were able to buy a house in Kings Langley where our kids were able to grow up. With a combination of generous gifts, an early inheritance, a mortgage offer that should never have been approved, we did find our dwelling place. Now every time we move to a new home, this sign comes with us as a reminder of His faithful provision. God gave us a home. Moriah – My God will provide!

We read the biblical story of Moriah and God's provision to Abraham in Genesis 22 from verse 1 onwards. Let us read this passage:

> Sometime later God tested Abraham. He said to him, "Abraham!" "Here I am," Abraham replied. [2]Then God said, "Take your son, your only son, whom you love—Isaac—and go to the region of Moriah. Sacrifice him there as a burnt offering on a mountain I will show you."

Abraham was entering a time of testing. God asked Abraham to surrender His dream of a future, the very hope of his life, and yield it back to God. He was asked to take this sacrificial gift, his son, to a very specific place, called Moriah, which means God will provide. So, as we read on, we discover Abraham is quick to obey:

> [3]Early the next morning Abraham got up and loaded his donkey. He took with him two of his servants and his son Isaac. When he had cut enough wood for the burnt offering, he set out for the

> place God had told him about. ⁴On the third day Abraham looked up and saw the place in the distance. ⁵He said to his servants, "Stay here with the donkey while I and the boy go over there. We will worship and then we will come back to you."

This moment for Abraham is like ripping a sticking plaster off your skin when it has become well and truly stuck. There is only one way to deal with the impending pain: do it quickly! Abraham realises that this is a tough test and, if he does not respond immediately, he may not respond at all. Obedience is often sacrificial, and it does hurt at some level. So Abraham gets up early the next morning, prepares all he needs, and starts this journey of obedience and sacrifice. His actions remind me of those times when God speaks to me about giving a sacrificial financial gift. If I lie in bed rationalising about the necessity of this gift, I will quickly talk myself out of obedience. When in this place, I find I need to get out of my bed quickly, write the cheque, transfer the money, act in obedience then and there, before I lose the courage to trust.

> ⁶Abraham took the wood for the burnt offering and placed it on his son Isaac, and he himself carried the fire and the knife. As the two of them went on together, ⁷Isaac spoke up and said to his father Abraham, "Father?". "Yes, my son?", Abraham replied. "The fire and wood are here," Isaac said, "but where is the lamb for the burnt offering?". ⁸Abraham answered, "God himself will provide the lamb for the burnt offering, my son." And the two of them went on together.

When you are walking through these tests of faith, it can be difficult to answer the well-meaning questions from family and friends. Unknowingly, Isaac touches the core issue that Abraham himself is having to reconcile as he walks with his son to Moriah. Will God provide a way of escape? Can He trust God with his hopes and dreams? In response to the questions, Abraham boldly declares that God will provide for them and they walk on.

> [9]When they reached the place God had told him about, Abraham built an altar there and arranged the wood on it. He bound his son Isaac and laid him on the altar, on top of the wood. [10]Then he reached out his hand and took the knife to slay his son. [11]But the angel of the LORD called out to him from heaven, "Abraham! Abraham!" "Here I am," Abraham replied.[12]"Do not lay a hand on the boy," he said. "Do not do anything to him. Now I know that you fear God, because you have not withheld from me your son, your only son."

They finally reach the place of reckoning, where God tests the trust and obedience of Abraham's heart. God gives Abraham very specific instructions, which he obeys, even though these orders seem to destroy the very gift of God's hope given to him. Just when it all looks hopeless, God speaks. He says, "Now I know you hope in me, so I can provide for you." Then we read the following:

> [13]Abraham looked up and there in a thicket he saw a ram caught by its horns. He went over and took the ram and sacrificed it as a burnt offering instead of his son. [14]So Abraham called that place The LORD Will Provide. And to this day it is said, "On the mountain of the LORD it will be provided."

In the midst of this severe and terrible test, God suddenly speaks and provides! Abraham had thought that he needed to provide the offering, his son, but now he sees the lamb that God has provided for this offering. Abraham had thought he needed to provide the sacrifice but instead he is able to hug his son once again and then declares, "My God does provide!" He has passed the test on Mount Moriah, he knows the full extent of God's provision. Abraham comes to a place of faith, hope and confidence that God will provide even the means to be obedient in this trial of faith. God provided everything. This is an amazing revelation.

PROVIDING FOR GOD OR NOT!

In the early years of our marriage I was not married to a pastor but a business man. Gordon and I had started a business with the vision to provide funds for various church projects. We felt excited at the prospect of making money for the Kingdom of God. We would provide the finance to enable others to get the work done. We were hope filled and excited. However, very quickly our business ended up in the High Court and we were involved in various legal challenges. Fortunately, all of them were resolved amicably, in the end. (The full story is told in Gordon's book called "Harnessed for Adventure", which you can buy on Amazon books – a great read!).

But as we encountered these various challenges in our business we learned several real-life lessons. Firstly, we recognised our naïve arrogance that we were going to provide for God and His work. We soon realised that it is God who is always the provider, but we do get to partner with him in the finance division. Secondly, God takes responsibility for His projects. What God orders, He is able to pay for! It is not our role to carry the heavy responsibility to find the money and pay the bills for God's projects. We do not provide for His work, He provides for us as we partner with Him. Lastly, we discovered that God was more interested in working on the lessons of hope and faith in our lives than He was in our ability to produce money for Him. God wanted us to learn this: He is always the source of our wealth! We need to remember this, as this scripture reminds us:

> But remember the Lord your God, for it is he who gives you the ability to produce wealth, and so confirms his covenant, which he swore to your ancestors, as it is today.
> **— DEUTERONOMY 8:18**

It is God who gives you the power to give. He is always the resource of everything we have. He is the one who empowers us to make money, it is not just our good business practice. When we start a business or give generously to God's work, we can be tempted to believe that we are now providing for the work of God ourselves. We need to have this revelation, as Abraham did, that God is always able to provide for Himself. We are not running the business to provide for God but rather we have the privilege to work with God in His kingdom business and watch the stories of a God of provision unfold. There is nothing more rewarding than watching God and business people work together to bring change into communities and lives.

PARTNERING WITH
THE GOD OF PROVISION

Since our business days, Gordon and I have pastored churches, been missionaries in Africa and served in Oxford. We have birthed ministries and found again and again that our hope in God has been richly rewarded. God has supplied more than our needs and used Gordon, especially, to be a source of hope to others as they have believed God for financial resources. Let's read Gordon's story of hope to encourage us to trust in this God of provision. Gordon writes:

> I remember back in 2012, God challenged me to birth a national movement called Mahabba, focussed on reaching out to Muslim people, out of what had initially started as a local church prayer meeting here in Oxford. At the time I regularly met with an accountability group of five men, and we used to share our lives and pray about our future adventures together. So I shared this recent God challenge with them, asking them for advice about how I was supposed to start a national movement with no money. I felt confused, as I really had very little hope of launching this movement with no funds.

One of the men in the group immediately laughed and said, "That's no problem! If this call is from God, then He will multiply whatever seed we sow in faith right now. Let's start by sowing a seed of £5 and watch to see what God does with it!" Someone threw a £5 note in the middle of the table and we all laid our hands on it and committed it to the Lord. I think the angels must have thought, "Wow, this is going to be fun to watch!" The next day I had to attend another prayer meeting and, at the end of the meeting, someone came up to me and put £50 in my hands, explaining that God had told him to give me this gift! Hope was beginning to rise – God was up to something! That evening I arrived home and shared this with Rachel, and to my surprise she said, "Let me take this to the next level – here's £500 for Mahabba." The next morning I was absolutely blown away to open a letter from a friend who hadn't contacted me for many years: out from the envelope dropped a cheque for £5000! God was multiplying the seed!

Now I was getting the message: God had a plan and I needed to get ready to work! I rented an office in Oxford and began to make plans with another friend to lay the foundations for launching this national movement called Mahabba. To my amazement, very shortly after this step of faith of obtaining the offices, I was sent a donation from an American foundation which was the rough equivalent of £50,000. Mahabba was launched that December 2012 and rapidly spread to about 75 cities in the UK as well as igniting Mahabba movements in other countries globally. After 7 years, I was able to hand over the leadership to other mission leaders but, what moved me so much, was realising that God had released slightly over £500,000 to us over those years, from many different Christian trusts and foundations.

Now serving in a consultancy role, I find myself working along-side the leadership of a Christian ministry who are building a brand-new HQ building which was budgeted to cost about £5 million. This connection sparked after we spent a weekend away together, with all their leaders, to pray over this project. During a time of communion, as we broke bread and sought God together, I suddenly found myself saying, "I've got faith for £5 million!" Where on earth did such a bold statement of hope come from? God had just dropped that seed gift of faith into my heart as we prayed! Together, as a team, we have already watched God supernaturally provide over £6 million. (Unfortunately the costs have increased significantly since the pre-Covid estimates!) God has provided in so many wonderful ways, through individuals, trust funds, companies and the generosity of ordinary people, far beyond our dreams. So now we stand hope filled - ready to trust Him for the final £2 million. God is so good, and He certainly has ways of inspiring your hope beyond all reason!

HOPE FILLED PROVISION FOR YOU AND YOUR CHILDREN

I wonder if you know this scripture in Genesis where Joseph speaks to his family after a long time of separation. We read this story in the book of Genesis.

> [20]"You intended to harm me, but God intended it for good to accomplish what is now being done, the saving of many lives. [21]So then, don't be afraid. I will provide for you and your children." And he reassured them and spoke kindly to them. [22]Joseph stayed in Egypt, along with all his father's family. He lived a hundred and ten years.
>
> **— GENESIS 50:20-22**

Joseph had just been reunited with his family after a time of separation that lasted about twenty two years. The journey to this point had not been great! His eldest brother, Reuben, had tried to kill him at 17 years old, and then all his brothers had lied about what had happened. Now here they were, reunited because of a time of great hardship and famine. Desperation had driven them back together. But Joseph did not accuse them of their past but asked them to see how God had used all these circumstances to position him to provide help for his family. Joseph was able to see God's story of hope, even through the last years of hardship, and choose to forgive. In a time of great trouble and famine, God reconnected this family and Joseph became the supplier of their needs. When they had no hope, they discovered God had already planned a way of hope for them.

I believe that God uses us, within our families, to be a beacon of hope in times of trouble. After times of betrayal and difficulty, we have amazing opportunities to open the door of hope to our siblings, parents and others who are hurting.

When we were missionaries for eight years, we often faced financial needs. We would pray, trust, hoping that God would supply again. So often God used Gordon's parents to bless us. They would just "happen" to send us a "random gift" which was the perfect amount for our need. This happened so regularly, it amazed us. At that time they would not have understood prayer and listening to God at any personal level but frequently it was their cheque that saved us and answered our cry for help! Sometimes we do not realise that God has blessed us to be an answer to the hope of others. We have been given wealth and resources to help our families and children in their time of need. God wants us to be like Him, a generous beacon of hope in times of hardship. We need to listen and ask God to train us to be ready to respond and serve Him as bearers of hope in difficult days.

ACTIVATION

Let's stop for a moment and consider this God who provides.

Do you know Moriah and this testing place of sacrifice in your financial life?

Can you recognise the steps of obedience you need to make in this time of testing?

Write them down.

Are you trying to provide for God...or do you partner with Him as He provides?

Pray and ask God to show you where you have taken wrong responsibility financially.

Finally, can you see how this God of provision is writing a story of hope for you and your family? Reflect for a while on the story of Joseph and then give God thanks.

GOD PROVIDES FOR
PRACTICAL NEEDS TOO

Our hope in God and for His provision should stretch from expecting Him to provide for our everyday practical needs as well as the large multi-million-pound projects. God is ready to provide for us at every level of life. Here are some scriptures to encourage you:

> You care for the land and water it; you enrich it abundantly. The streams of God are filled with water to provide the people with corn, for so you have ordained it.
> **— PSALM 65:9**

> You provide a broad path for my feet, so that my ankles do not
> give way.
> **— PSALM 18:36**

When God created this world, He planned even the water cycle with care so that we would be able to grow our food and eat. He also provides us with a secure path in life, giving us a safe place to walk, where we will not stumble and fall. God wants us to see that His provision goes far beyond money. He wants us to understand that He desires to take care of every need that affects our wellbeing, health and life too. Our hope in God's provision must go beyond our bank balance. We need to grasp the reliability of our God, who is so trustworthy, providing for us in such intimate and detailed ways. We can trust Him even when the stream of provision we have been promised has stagnated, and help seems to be far away.

UNBLOCKING THE
WELLS OF PROVISION

Here is a wonderful testimony of God's power and care. Read and enjoy!

When you came to The Ark recently for our special gathering, you brought a word about unblocking the stagnation around your rightful inheritances. At that time, we had three properties that were all "blocked" and totally stagnated, and you prayed specifically with myself and my wife. We needed a breakthrough. We have been holding onto His word through you and we thought you may like to know that He has now answered our prayers.

Last Saturday, we had an offer on a house that had been on the market for a year.

Yesterday, we exchanged contracts on the sale of my late father's house, and we will complete the sale next Friday. That sale has been dragging its heels for months.

Today, we received news that the insurance company has accepted liability for a subsidence claim that has been ongoing since January. Remedial work starts on Monday.

So all three of these stagnated situations are now unblocked and unblocked in the same week! He is a faithful God. Many blessings to you, and many thanks for the hope you have given us over the last few weeks.

Thank you
— Richard H

YES! What a wonderful story of hope and provision! Our God provides and cares.

HOPE FOR THE FUTURE

We started this chapter by reflecting on the way our financial security can also alter our perspective concerning our future. As we become more secure in God to provide for every area of our lives, we should also be prepared to experience a fresh spiritual urgency concerning the future. As hope is rekindled, and our sense of destiny stirred, we suddenly begin to believe we can make a difference in this world. Hope is restored and we can think about tomorrow again. When we are living in the prison of financial lack and fear, we have no capacity to dream about tomorrow; we are simply fighting to survive today! But as hope rises and we trust God to provide today, we begin to dream again.

I believe that God is calling many of you to hope in Him again. He is calling you to draw near to Him and follow His way. We read this call to the early disciples in Mark's gospel:

> "Come, follow me," Jesus said, "and I will send you out to fish for people."
> — **MARK 1:17**

Jesus is calling you, "Come up higher into a new level of trust concerning my call upon your life and the provision I have for you." As we give our lives to follow Jesus afresh in this way, He gives us fresh purpose. He asks us to join Him on an adventure, sharing with people our assurance in God. Jesus asks us to carry His message of hope to those in debt, overwhelmed with fear and anxiety concerning money, and show them how Jesus can change every mess into a message of hope.

God is changing your perspective, helping you know he has a secure future for you, and He will give you a message to share. Get ready to write your story of HOPE!

ACTIVATION

Allow God to show you where you trust him easily for His provision, and then where you need to learn to trust Him more. Write this down.

Are there stagnated areas of provision that need to be unblocked? Ask for Holy Spirit's strategy to unblock these situations.

Finally, ask God to renew your vision of your future, free from the fear of money.

Can you hear the call of God – COME!

Pray and reflect.

7

HOPE FILLED

For our friends and families

> "There is always hope."
> **— ARAGORN, THE LORD OF THE RINGS**

Jesus is my hope for my health, wealth and my relationships too. We have explored the health and wealth issues and now we come to the secret garden of our lives. This is the inner sanctuary of our hopes and dreams. As children we all imagine our wedding day, or that moment of watching dad's face fill with pride when we win the race at sports' day, or the joy of receiving an academic prize at college in front of friends and family. Wired within our being is the longing for happy, secure, fun loving relationships with our spouse, children, and friends. So many of our hopes are anchored right here, in our relationships.

Is there still hope if we discover that our husband is having an affair, our best friend betrays our trust, our children are experimenting with drugs, or our family is feuding about money? What are the foundation stones of our hope in God for the family and how do we hold this ground? I love this quote above from the Lord of the Rings: "There is always hope!".

I grew up in a Christian home and went to church before I was born! I have always known Jesus' way and implicitly trusted that Jesus would take care of my home and kids. I was not a mum who was fearful about my children but as Nicola and David, our two children, approached their teenage years, I began to worry. This fear was seeded in my mind after a random conversation during a coffee morning with some church girls. They turned to me and asked, "Rachel, aren't you worried now your kids are becoming teenagers? You know what kids are like these days. I wonder if they will cope with being a pastor's kid or rebel like most kids do? Do you think they will try drugs? After all, pastors' kids are notorious for being the ones to cause trouble in their teens and you travel so much. Don't you worry about them?" This casual conversation seeded fear in my heart. I suddenly thought to myself, maybe I was being naïve. Maybe something was happening, and I had not noticed it. Once I got home I began to pray, not good prayers but anxious, worry filled prayers! These frantic prayers further compounded the anxiety I had allowed into my heart. I then found myself scrutinizing my kids' faces more closely, looking in their bedrooms for any tell-tell signs; I was becoming fear driven. I would never have considered myself to be "one of those" mums. But here I was, eaten up with worry about my kids, and for no apparent reason. They were good kids!

I was away again, travelling to Manchester for a weekend of ministry and, as I walked into the conference hall, a friend I knew stopped me and asked to speak with me privately. As soon as we were alone she said to me, "Rachel, God woke me up and told me to come today and speak with you!" She went on to explain that God had given her a dream. In it I was standing with my heart exposed and I was allowing the enemy to wound my hope and confidence concerning my kids and family. She then began to pray, "Father, today I uproot every word, all idle chatter, that has stripped Rachel's defences of peace. Right now we tear down every lie of the enemy that He has planted into your soul." Then she hugged me and said, "Rachel, do not let your fears make false appointments for your kids. God holds your kids, He has got your home. Do not fear!" In that moment everything changed and a confident hope for my kids returned. They were born to love God and they would not waver. I was back on my front foot again. What a wicked devil!

WE WILL SERVE THE LORD

> But if serving the LORD seems undesirable to you, then choose for yourselves this day whom you will serve, whether the gods your ancestors served beyond the Euphrates, or the gods of the Amorites, in whose land you are living. But as for me and my household, we will serve the LORD.
> **— JOSHUA 24:15**

This familiar scripture quoted above, "As for me and my house, we will serve the LORD!", is often used as the foundation of our prayers for the family. It simply states that we hope our home will be one that chooses to stay together and love Jesus. We instinctively know that we need to be a God centred household if we are to flourish. This statement of hope is the longing of our hearts concerning our families. God, let us make good choices and keep you in the centre. Many mothers have prayed this scripture earnestly over their children as they have begun to make alternative choices for their lives. God's word breathes life into those moments of challenge in the family. He gives us hope for the marriage that is failing, the children who have abandoned church, and family members who do not agree with your stand for Jesus. Our hope for our family's salvation is rooted in many scriptures like this one which encourage us to believe that God will be in our homes. There are choices, intentional, positive decisions that we need to make to set the compass of our home on the ways of God. "Choose this way" is our deepest cry of hope!

Many of our prayers for the relationships in our homes and community are centred on this hope that they will turn to Jesus who will save, restore and reconcile them. We pray that people in our world will make this choice. We can see the pain of the relational fall out of wounded people who are not walking with God and, as we pray, God fills us with hope that He can turn around these desperate situations. The Bible says in Luke that one of the purposes of the coming of Jesus was to turn people's hearts around. Let us read this scripture for ourselves:

> And he will go on before the Lord, in the spirit and power of Elijah, to turn the hearts of the parents to their children and the disobedient to the wisdom of the righteous—to make ready a people prepared for the Lord.
> **— LUKE 1:17**

As we meditate on these promises, we find hope to pray for the walls between parents and their children to be removed and a melting of hearts to occur. Whatever the relational fallout we have experienced, Jesus has come to bring us hope and a new atmosphere so that true relationships can grow back healed.

HEARTS TURNED TO JOY

Why don't we take a moment to read this wonderful story of God's kindness to a mother and her daughter? He has restored their hearts. My friend writes:

At the Women's Retreat for our church, I spoke with you on the second night about something you had mentioned during your session. I told you about my struggle with my sweet daughter, and you gave me very good counsel.

As you suggested, I prayed over my daughter as she slept for several weeks. I prayed that He would break off a spirit of resentment, anger, selfishness, rage, jealousy – in Jesus' name. As I continued, I realised that the Lord was revealing to me that I should be asking Him to do that for me, too! So, I did. I cannot begin to tell you the difference in the atmosphere in our home and our lives. The Lord is so faithful! Our relationship is the sweetest it has ever been, and I can't wait to see how the Lord will continue to deepen our love for one another as mother and daughter.

While praying soon after this time, I felt the Lord giving me a new name for her – Joy! She loves this name (although I still call her by her first name too). While we were camping soon after this breakthrough, my daughter was wearing a shirt and a jacket that had a peace sign on them. I told her, "Do you know what often comes with joy? Peace!" And she replied, "Well, maybe that is my brother's real name! We are Peace and Joy!" I was overwhelmed when I heard her say that. Here was my daughter speaking about her brother in this way after all the trauma of the anger and jealousy we had previously experienced.

I hope this encourages your heart, wherever you are! Thank you again, Rachel. From the bottom of my heart, I believe that God in you has given me my daughter back! God be praised for his indescribable gifts! Much love, CL.

JESUS MY ONLY HOPE

And when I am lifted up from the earth, I will draw everyone to myself!

— **JOHN 12:32**

Jesus has a distinctive. He is unique. He needs to be displayed for all to see. We need to learn how to lift up this name of Jesus in our family, friendships and work spaces so that people are able to see what we know. Let the magnetic power of the name of Jesus draw people to Him. This is where our hope for the future of our communities is rooted.

We want people to know our Jesus who saves, who heals, and who delivers. This is a day of salvation for many, including those in our friendship groups and homes. We need to make Jesus plain for people to see. We need to be bold and pray for the sick and share the power of the name of Jesus and watch Him work miracles in their lives. We need to ask God for new levels of discernment so that we can identify the roots of torment in people's lives and break the bondages that hold them. There is so much shame, fear and emotional trauma in people's lives. We need to see the name of Jesus utterly deliver them. This is a day of freedom for our loved ones. Let your expectation arise. Even if you have prayed for years and nothing has seemed to change, I do believe this is a day of hope for our friends and family. This is a day of dreams coming true and families turning to God!

SALVATION COMES TO OUR HOUSE

Praying for a family member to turn to Jesus can be a laborious task. There can be so many highs and lows. In my experience, as often as you increase your level of prayer, life seems to upgrade its level of hassle. Praying seems to make things worse before they turn around! But when you watch someone in your family finally turn to Jesus, there is no joy like it, even if the path has been complicated! I have asked Gordon to share this story with you:

At the age of 14, I was so desperate to understand what life was all about that I became mesmerised by the teaching of an American cult which centred on keeping all the Jewish laws and festivals, without ever really coming to a living faith and trust in Jesus. I was so fanatical that I shared all my ideas with my elder brother who had just joined the British Army. As a result, he left the Army, enrolled in the Bible School of the cult, which had opened close to our home, and became a central part of their Church and community.

I, however, was rescued from the deceptive teaching of this cult by a young teacher at my school who had studied theology. He very lovingly walked through all the teachings of the cult with me, showing me their fundamental error. As a result, feeling so betrayed and wounded, I closed my heart to God, joined the Army and hated anything to do with religion, and later even took time out of my military service to go to Cambridge to seek to disprove all religion. God was so gracious to me, and I was saved through a personal encounter with Jesus during a revival in Cambridge in 1974.

Sadly, my brother stayed within the cult, even though our sister then became a believer during a Billy Graham Crusade. Throughout the next decades of our mission and ministry life, Rachel and I would regularly pray for my brother to have a revelation of Jesus but there was no indication that our prayers were making any difference. We have learned over the years that we cannot manipulate people through our prayers, as every person has their own free will to follow their conscience. Prayer does change atmospheres and situations, however, and recognises that "the God of this world has blinded the minds of non-believers". Our consistent prayer does enable the light of revelation to finally break through to people, but they still have the free will to choose their own path.

It must have been almost 30 years after my brother first joined this cult, and Rachel was leading prayer in our church in Watford. She shared how prayer was like putting up poles and stringing up another length of power cable from God towards a person or situation: you never know when the connection will finally be made! She asked each person to choose one "stubborn" prayer which seemed impossible and shared that today could be the final prayer before Heaven touched this resistant situation. The "stubborn" prayer we chose that night was praying once again for my brother, and we both dutifully prayed along with everyone else and went home.

To my amazement, later that week, my brother called our home and said he wanted to see me: he wanted to give his life to Jesus. His whole cult had been going through a time of re-education, and all their ministers had been sent to London Bible College to correct their theology about Jesus and salvation through the Cross. He had had an encounter with Jesus and, within a short space of time, he committed his life to serve in missions to the Jews. He soon became a missionary in the Ukraine, reaching out to the Russian Jews. Today he loves Jesus. God is so good!

ACTIVATION

Ask God to remind you of those you have prayed for over the years. Write down their names. Do you know their story today? What choices have they made?

Where do you need fresh hope for your friends and family? Write down the names of the friends and family you want to see turning towards God.

Ask God to stir hope for these prayer challenges!

Reflect with God on how your choices have shaped the course of your life over these years. Thank Him for the Jesus way and its blessings in your home and friendships!

JESUS ENCOUNTERS

> They said to the woman, "We no longer believe just because of what you said; now we have heard for ourselves, and we know that this man really is the Saviour of the world."
> — **JOHN 4:42**

Here is a woman who has a life changing encounter with Jesus at the well in her village and then proceeds to turn her community upside down. You may be familiar with this story that we read in John's Gospel. Jesus approaches the well with his disciples who then leave to go and buy bread in the village. This woman is a Samaritan and alone so, culturally, Jesus, as a Jew and a single man on his own, should not have engaged her in conversation. But He does! Jesus asks her to draw water from the well and give Him a drink; He then begins to talk to her about the thirst in her life for friendship. In this conversation, Jesus talks in depth with her about her loneliness and broken relationships revealing that she is thirsty for more. At first the woman defends herself but then quickly acknowledges that she has had many broken marriages and is now living with her partner but within her she carries deep longings. Jesus then reveals that He can fulfil these needs, as He carries everlasting water that satisfies the cry of the human heart. She receives this water of life and makes the choice to drink. In an instant she knows her life has been transformed. The disciples return from their shopping trip and are perplexed by what they see. But nothing is going to dampen the excitement of this encounter for this woman: she is fully alive and she cannot keep silent. Her joy was so infectious that others around her immediately noticed the change. They could see she had encountered life and became hungry too.

In the passage I quoted above, we read the conclusion to the story and this wonderful confession of her friends. They come to find this woman and tell her, "your changed life had such a profound impact on us that we have now gone on our own journey. We have found Jesus for ourselves. We are not only excited about your story, we have our own story now. Jesus has changed our lives too!" What a powerful encounter. I pray that expectancy awakens in our hearts for our friends and colleagues in the workplace. God, let encounters happen all around us and turn people's lives upside down!

JESUS RESCUES US

> He who redeems your life from the pit and crowns you with love and compassion.
> **— PSALM 103:4**

Jesus not only saves you from your past and the pit of hopelessness, but He also redeems your future. He restores your life, pays off the debt, and sets you free for a future of hope.God has a total rescue plan for our lives.

This redeeming work of Jesus can make any life hope filled again. The blood of Jesus has the power to make us clean. It removes the marks of the past and rewires our inner thinking and reactions to respond to God's way. The Bible uses the picture of being cleansed until we are as white as snow. This means a pure, sparkling white heart – better than any laundry advert! The blood of Jesus restores you to wholeness and removes all shame and guilt. It is transformational. His life changes everything.

My favourite type of church service is the baptism. In this service people who have recently given their life to Jesus decide to publicly acknowledge their decision by stepping into a tank of water, completely immersing themselves to represent the washing away of their past life, and then stepping out into a new way of life, washed and clean. I love this powerful imagery. I love watching the joy on their faces as they realise that Jesus has rescued them. I love seeing the sparkle of new hope in their eyes. But the very best part is listening to the stories of hope in Jesus. Before each person steps into the water, they tell a little part of their story that brought them to God.

Recently, a young woman in one of our baptismal services shared her story. She had first attended church almost by accident, not realising what she would encounter when her friends had invited her to come. She had been longing for a child and a family but had struggled to conceive. She was now a few weeks pregnant. During the service she had gone to the bathroom. Noticing that she had begun to bleed, she became fearful that she would lose her child. Going back into the service, she had decided to ask God to help. "God, please let me have this child and I will give you my life completely and dedicate the life of my child to you." That evening as she told this story, she was baptised with tears flowing down her face; she held her son in her arms, with her husband by her side, as they thanked God for the new life in their home. God had rescued her life, given her a son, and completely changed their home.

Every life has a rescue story which demonstrates a different aspect of the love of God. Jesus rescues all, and there is hope for the hardest heart!

HOPING AGAINST HOPE AGAIN

What about those relationships with people in our world who choose not to walk with Jesus? We all have individuals in our lives who are friends or family members, whom we love and have long-term relational conections with, who push back on our faith. How do we legitimately carry our hope when relating to these people? Is there still hope when a marriage you prayed about for years suddenly ends? What happens to your hope then? As we have already seen in this chapter, people have to make their own choices. God did not make us as puppets, with strings of control so that we can only do what He says, but rather He calls us to be partners, willingly offering our lives to walk with Him. So what happens if we turn to Jesus but our spouse, family member or close friend decides that this Jesus life is not for them? God respects their choice. We can pray that they will change their mind, and many times they will, but sometimes I have seen people harden their hearts and make definite decisions to turn away from God. This is hard. But God still has a way for you. This is another of those messy life situations where we have to let our earthly hopes wrestle with our eternal hope and leave God to sort out the mess!

I remember God's gracious kindness to a woman I met at a conference. This is her story of hope in the midst of hopelessness:

As I began to speak at a conference, God gave me a word for a woman. I saw her standing in a large house with lots of children, and I shared with her that God was going to open doors for her to be a mother to the fatherless of our society. God was opening doors for her to touch the hearts of broken children with love and hope. As I spoke this word over her life, I could see that she was deeply moved and that it resonated with her heart. After the session, she came and found me and asked me to pray. She said I had described her desires exactly. She wanted to go out to Romania, or a nation like that, and open a home to take care of children that were lonely and without family. However, her husband was not yet saved and did not want anything to do with this type of project. We prayed.

It must have been about two years later before I heard the next part of this story. Six weeks after my word, this woman had returned home after work to find a letter saying her husband had decided to leave her and their two boys. She was devastated and wondered how this word could now be true. The next six months were painful. She tried to be a single parent to her boys and help them navigate the loss of their dad, while sorting out her finances and her life for the future. Everything felt overwhelming. One day, the head of year of her son's class at school asked to see her. She was concerned as she went to the appointment: maybe her boy was not coping at school either. However, the meeting turned out to be a total surprise. The head of year expressed her sympathy about the recent break up of the marriage but then asked this mum what tools she was using to help her boys as they appeared remarkably well grounded emotionally considering how recently their father had left home. This mum then shared how she was talking to her boys honestly about the loss, training them in values and attitudes of forgiveness, and showing them how to express their emotions well. The teacher then asked the mum if she would consider taking an after school class to help other boys who were growing up in single parent homes too. This woman walked out of the meeting stunned. She went home, prayed, then felt she should respond and say yes. To cut a long story short, this precious mum went on to hold many after school clubs for children who had lost a parent. Then, one day, the council contacted her. "We have a house we would like to offer you for the use of helping these children from difficult family situations. Would you be interested in running a centre for them?" Here she was about to sign a contract for a house to give a home to children who were fatherless and needing care. God had done a miracle and she was now realising her hopes and dreams, albeit in a very different way and under different circumstances to what she had imagined.

Even when life looks hopeless, God can find a way for you!

ALL THINGS NEW

As you read this chapter and reflect on these testimonies, I pray that you will experience a renewed sense of anticipation for your relationships. Often we can despair, wondering if their stubborn hearts will ever yield. But let hope arise for their salvation. In this season I believe that many prodigal children will run home and embrace Jesus again. The stalemate will come to an end. God delights to give us new things – a new start – a new name - new perspective and so the list could continue. In fact there are 192 references in the Bible that use the word new!

In this season that feels difficult, get ready for the new harvest. We read this verse in Leviticus:

> You will still be eating last year's harvest when you will have to move it out to make room for the new.
> **— LEVITICUS 26:10**

God is able to make all things new. He is a God of change and we will find that suddenly we will need to shift our normal to make room for the new things happening in our relationships. I remember chatting to a wife who was still coming to terms with her husband's new outlook on life and her children's faith. She was laughing and explaining, "I don't know how to plan anymore! I keep thinking we will stay at home and have an easy night, only to discover that my family has already arranged to serve at a church meeting. I cannot get used to their new excitement and desire to be with people. We used to have a quiet life and a very slow pace – now everyone is going in all directions. Their new passion for Jesus has changed everything!" Everything was new!

TURNING GENERATIONS

We also need to understand the legacy of God's hope expressed through families. Often it takes one person to find Jesus and then, through their influence and witness, the rest of the family find Jesus too and suddenly there is a new generational flow, a spiritual legacy being crafted by the next generations. I call this first person who turns to Jesus, the "turning generation". They are the ones who bring hope to their family by being the first in their family line to turn to Christ. They turn the generational flow of their family towards God by choosing Jesus. Their influence of life and the power of their prayer then softens the hearts of others until they bring hope into their homes. Often the first person who takes a stand for Jesus in their family has a tough time. They can feel alone, misunderstood and isolated in their faith. They feel the heat of the turning. If you imagine a huge supertanker at sea suddenly stopping in its tracks, and then making a full 180 degree turn, you would see the turbulence in the water. This is what is feels like spiritually for the one who stops a godless generational flow and turns it around for Jesus. It causes some waves! But as you persist and turn and find the new direction, the water will settle and you will again move forward, full steam ahead. So if you are the pivot point in your generation, do not give up! Keep turning the flow and watch what Jesus will create in your family.

This is a prayer that I have claimed for my family and its line. This is the generational blessing that I believe we can expect. So why not take this scripture and pray it for your home and family too:

> "As for me, this is my covenant with them," says the LORD. "My Spirit, who is on you, will not depart from you, and my words that I have put in your mouth will always be on your lips, on the lips of your children and on the lips of their descendants—from this time on and forever," says the LORD.
> — **ISAIAH 59:21**

LEAVING A LEGACY OF HOPE

I was talking with my uncle at a family celebration when I discovered a thread of God's grace running through my Dad's family line that I had never known. My great-granny was an amazing woman! I had often heard about this great-granny, who had prayed for my Dad and had given him a Bible in his late teens when he was a self-proclaimed atheist, but I had never understood her story. Here is the story I was told:

My great-granny lived in the Rhonda valley, in Wales. She was married with five children and had a hard life providing for this family. One of her children was Stanley, my grandfather. Her husband worked in the mines and life was tough. Like most in the community, they would attend chapel on Sundays and were God-fearing people without a personal relationship with God. But at this time in Wales,

God was awakening these little chapels and their communities through the preaching of Evan Roberts and the Welsh revival. Hope was stirring in the hearts of many Welsh homes. One hopeless day, feeling overwhelmed, my great-granny was sitting in a field, with her apron still round her waist, feeling desperate. She was losing hope. The money was short, her marriage tough with a husband who liked his drink, and her growing family was rowdy. As she sat trying to find a moment's peace, the sound of singing filled her ears. "Here is love vast as the ocean....", the hymn of the Welsh revival. As these words floated up the valley to the field where she sat, she asked God to show her this love.

My great-granny had an encounter with Jesus and from that moment became a woman of prayer and faith. She began to pray for her husband and her five children. As the children began to marry and have children, each grandchild also became a target of prayer on her list. My Dad, Alan, spoke about how his granny challenged him to love Jesus and read the Bible. But my Dad was not interested in these things at this time and politely ignored all her prompts. As far as we are aware, not much changed in the faith life of the family while great-granny was alive. She prayed faithfully but her children and grandchildren remained stubbornly independent. But then something happened!

My Dad, now married and a very capable chemist, moved to Nottingham where he began to lecture at the university. There a work colleague began to ask him if he had a faith in God. At the same time Mormon missionaries knocked on my parents' door, wanting to talk about their beliefs. Dad was interested in moving to America so he was willing to listen to their chatter for a short while, only if he could then ask questions about America. But all this was a set up! Billy Graham was coming to London and dad's work friend invited him to go. Behind the scenes their prayer group began to pray for Dad. The Mormons began to talk about their religion and Dad remembered enough from his church days to know something was different. He needed a Bible to read to prove this. So Dad went up into the attic to find his granny's Bible. He began to read. He prepared himself and found he was able to enjoy his debating sessions with the Mormons. But then he began to realise that he was enjoying reading the Bible more. This book was powerful! My Dad found himself being captivated by the words of the pages of this book. Researching for his conversations with these Mormon boys was becoming more fun than he thought. He began to think about God. He then began to question his friend at work about things he did not understand until his work colleague arranged for Dad to go and see a man called Gordon Penny. Now Dad found a man who could answer his theological questions but also challenge him on the issues of his heart. Dad found himself being drawn to this person of Jesus, while Mum watched in surprise. Finally Gordon Penny asked Dad if he would surrender his life to God. My Dad was ready and he prayed and gave God everything. Mum then followed Dad's decision and surrendered her heart too.

Over the next few years, Dad's brother came to Jesus. Mum's sisters came to Jesus and this family turned to God. Mum and Dad have three children, and all of us love Jesus. My parents have seven grandchildren; they all love Jesus too and now they have six great-grandchildren, all starting their journey of faith. So when I think about my great-grandmother and her investment of prayer and the gift of that Bible to my Dad, I wonder if she could ever have known the tsunami of God's grace that would be released upon us, five generations later, because she prayed and gave. She died not knowing any of this story. Her grandson was still a hardened rebel against God but everything changed! There is hope, beyond our hope, that we cannot see or understand yet. So continue to pray and give and let God write your story of hope too!

TIME TO CREATE MEMORIES

One of the most beautiful things about long-term friendships or families is having the opportunities to remember and celebrate together. The opportunity to honour and look back at dreams fulfilled is precious. Days of celebration, when we intentionally tell the stories of hopes fulfilled, missions accomplished, and lives lived well are so important. Here we see that this was encouraged by God too. We read in the book of Joshua about the children of Israel when they crossed over the River Jordan and survived another difficulty, seeing God do miracles. Let us read the story:

> ⁶We will use these stones to build a memorial. In the future your children will ask you, "What do these stones mean?" Then you can tell them, ⁷"They remind us that the Jordan River stopped flowing when the Ark of the LORD's Covenant went across." These stones will stand as a memorial among the people of Israel forever.
> — **JOSHUA 4:6-7 (NLT)**

I believe that it is so important that we rehearse the stories of hope that we carry in our families and use them to stir the curiosity of our children about God. Mark special days and use them to provoke your kids to ask you about what they mean. I took my family out for a special meal, in a beautiful restaurant, on 27 October 2014. The kids were surprised and wondered what the occasion was. They knew it was not a birthday or anniversary but they could not remember the significance of this date. Just before the event David, my son, remembered my accident and the fact that I had almost died. Suddenly, the family realised, this was celebrating 30 years of life. We had such a special evening celebrating all the adventures of God that we had experienced as a family because I had lived. We marked the day, built a memorial and gave thanks. But I also noticed that after that evening there was a new expectation in our family for miracles and a new engagement to press into our God given dreams. Hope was kindled. The quote from Lord of the Rings is so right for families – "There is always hope!" More hope than we can ever realise.

ACTIVATION

What are the new things you want to see in your relationships? Dream and hope.

Who was the turning person in your family line? Do you know? Was it you?

Thank God for this person, including you!

Consider how you can set up some memory moments in your life.

Give thanks for the hopes and dreams that have been accomplished.

8

HOPE FILLED

For the nations and our world

"Hope for the best but prepare for the worst."
— **ENGLISH PROVERB**

"Hope sees the invisible, feels the intangible and achieves the impossible."
— **CHARLES COLTON**

Now let's look at the challenge of living a hope filled life in a hopeless world. If you were to believe everything that you read, you would understand by now that you will soon drown, fry, or starve! There is not much hope for a long, happy life according to the press. You will drown because the ice cap is melting and soon the British Isles will be completely under water; you will fry because of the heatwaves and raging fires; or starve due to the global grain shortage and lack of food. Not much hope here. Although I do not want to trivialise the complex issues in the nations due to war and climate change, we do need to remember a different worldview: God designed this world and He still has the last word. So breathe, laugh and enjoy life.

You will notice from the two quotes above very different outlooks on life. The good old English proverb demonstrates our natural inclination to be cautious and negative. It almost confirms the underlying fear: please get ready for tough days, prepare for the worst in the midst of your hope! Whereas the other quote expresses the principle that hope needs to look up and see the greater opportunities, and believe in what is as yet unseen.

JESUS – HOPE FOR MY WORLD

What is the basis for our hope in these days, living in such an uncertain world? Jesus! The Bible makes a clear statement that Jesus is our hope for the nations. We read this scripture in Matthew:

> In his name the nations will put their hope.
> — **MATTHEW 12:21**

As we study our communities around us and read the statistics of people's lives in our nations, we quickly become aware of a great sense of hopelessness. There are many contributors to this narrative: the economic challenges – bankrupt businesses - rising interest rates – falling house prices – diminishing pensions – failing health - broken families – shattered marriages – drugs, alcohol and other addictions – violence and stabbings on our streets. The list of heartaches experienced around us seems relentless. Although government and other institutions have their part to play in solving these crises, the ultimate answer is with the church. We need to share the hope we have in Jesus. There is no other way!

> Therefore, since we have such a hope, we are very bold.
> — **2 CORINTHIANS 3:12**

We need to allow this truth - Jesus is the hope for our world, our communities and our lives - to change the way we think. We need to let a new perspective of unashamed hope arise, be courageous, and seek to bring Jesus' values and attitudes into our culture. As Jesus people we have often felt intimidated and that we should hide the simplicity of our answer to these real life crises of hope. But now we must be bold for the sake of the nations.

We need to ask God to renew our attitudes and expectations and root them back in the word of God. Our outlook has been defined by the latest news bulletin, or liberal thinking concerning our truth - we need a new hope filled boldness. We need to hear that God has not finished with our nations yet. He has a game plan and even though we may seem beaten, we are on the home straight: God has saved the best till last!

Let us read this scripture from Jeremiah again but, this time, apply it to our nations. Our God is a God of hope for the micro details of our life and the macro details of our world. He holds all things together in His hands. As you read this scripture, make this a prayer for your community, region, and nation:

> "For I know the plans I have for you", declares the LORD, "plans to prosper you and not to harm you, plans to give you hope and a future."
> — **JEREMIAH 29:11**

ACTIVATION

Ask God to fill you with hope for your nation. Pray for a while.

"Oh God, we thank you that you have plans to prosper and give hope to our nation. Lord, keep our communities and people from harm. God, reveal your future for our nation. Amen."

Write down any scriptures or thoughts that God gives you as you pray.

OVERWHELMED OR ONE WHO OVERCOMES

We need our hope to be stirred and our expectation renewed concerning the state of our nations. We need to move from feeling overwhelmed to an overcoming confidence in the power of Jesus. In the book of Revelation we read this wonderful, triumphant statement of hope declared from the heavens:

> [10]Then I heard a loud voice in heaven say: "Now have come the salvation and the power and the kingdom of our God, and the authority of his Messiah. For the accuser of our brothers and sisters, who accuses them before our God day and night, has been hurled down. [11]They triumphed over him by the blood of the Lamb and by the word of their testimony; they did not love their lives so much, as to shrink from death."
> **— REVELATION 12:10-11**

There is another sound we need to hear. The sound of the proclamation of Heaven speaking about the power of our God and the defeat of the devil's accusation. All around us we can hear the constant negative narrative about people, officials and institutions. It is exhausting! We need to hear another story; a hope filled sound. We will not be beaten and overwhelmed but we will overcome and stand. We can be confident of this good outcome because the blood of Jesus has paid the price. There is also another powerful sound coming from the hearts and mouths of grateful people, sharing their good news story. We overcome this season of hopelessness by speaking about the power of Jesus' story in our life. All through this book I have been recounting stories of hope, true stories where people have found that God is more than enough to meet their cry. I believe that there are more stories of transformation about our nations that will also be written - a new record of history, where we tell HIS STORY in the nations!

So now get ready for another testimony of hope, one which reaches across the nations. Enjoy!

Hi Rachel,

I just thought I would send you a quick testimony from the service on Sunday. I hope it is a real encouragement to you. Thanks for coming.

C. is a Canadian guy, based in the UK, who has a very significant job in the music industry as a producer. He travels regularly to Nashville, USA, but has had some personal issues recently. He woke up Saturday morning, believing he had to go to church – just out of the blue. So he made a transatlantic phone call to a friend who suggested he come to KingsGate, Peterborough, where you were speaking that Sunday.

His friend in the USA assured him, "I have been praying for you for 15 months, God is going to really speak to you." C. pitches up to our second service, responds and stands at the front. Then you, Rachel, had a very significant word for him that he described as "reading my life like a book".

C. then went to the salvation room where BR led him into a full understanding of the difference between a knowledge of God and a heart relationship with Him. C. invited Jesus to be Lord of his life for the first time and cried like a baby!

He is now back off to Nashville this week but intends to be back in church as soon as he is back in the UK. Thank you, Lord!! Pastor TG

IT STARTS WITH A SEED

God woke me up with this phrase – "it starts with a seed" - early one morning. I had gone to bed thinking about the state of the nation and asking God how we should pray. Obviously these thoughts must have lingered in my heart all night long, so when I awoke, this phrase continued to resonate through my spirit, repeating again and again. "Rachel, it starts with a seed!" Finally, I could not sleep anymore and went downstairs to think and pray.

As I considered this statement further, I felt God say that He wants us to understand that we each carry His hope for the nations in seed form. He has given us His word. God has spoken to us about our families, communities and nations. Those words of promise and prophecy, which we hold dear, have life. They are the seeds that carry the legacy and DNA that will transform the hopelessness of society and turn it back to a land of hope and glory! All the gifts, creativity, inventions, and strategy necessary for the nations to flourish are carried in this seed form of His word and given to us to steward for the next generation. We have been given the seeds of hope for the nations.

I found myself mulling this thought over and over all day and felt that somehow this phrase felt familiar. Maybe I had heard it before somewhere? So I decided to google it and see. Immediately my search was rewarded. In Christ Church College, Oxford, a young man called William Penn had had an encounter with God while sitting in the library. William was discouraged as his hope for the future had been dealt a major blow since his dad had just lost the family estate whilst gambling. William's future expectations had radically changed in that moment. His family was bankrupt and now without their family home. He went to the King and asked for a reprieve but he was told the wager must stand and could not be reversed. However, the officials had pity on him and offered Penn an opportunity. They asked if he would be willing to go to the new territories of America and make a homestead there. These events had brought Penn to this place, where he was sitting in the library contemplating the choices ahead, when God spoke to him. Later Penn described the following statement as the call he received after this conversation with God:

"There may be room there for such a Holy Experiment, for the nations want a precedent and my God will make it the Seed of a Nation, that an example may be set up to the nations, that we may do the thing that is truly wise and just." William Penn

After this encounter Penn wasted no time and relocated to live on the land given to him. The rest is history, as they say. This land has become known as Pennsylvania and is still one of the American states today. But as Penn stated, this hope for Pennsylvania started as a seed after a time of hopelessness. God spoke to Penn who was willing to give his life to shape a new society, believing that this seed word of vision was enough to direct him.

I believe that God is looking for people of hope who recognise that this is the time for holy experiments once again. God is asking us to take hold of the seed words we have been given and give our lives sacrificially to the mission of turning hope into reality. As with Penn, it does not happen easily or quickly, but, in time, there is a legacy of a new community crafted into the nation - God's holy experiment that is wise and just at its heart.

As you consider this story, you may feel that you have neither seed nor hope and that everything is far too high for you to reach. But remember, Penn was bankrupt, with no means to fulfil his dream either. Where do we start?

We need to come and find a place to talk to God. Penn chose a library in Oxford. I don't know where your reflective place would be, but find a place and allow God to activate the hidden seed of hope in your heart. Why is prayer so important in moments like this? Prayer is the incubation chamber where God is able to agitate His seed. As you pray, you start a conversation with God. Penn received a clear mandate for his life and knew what to do. I believe that God can speak to you too. Remember, God has plans for your life and also plans for the nation. You may be standing at a crossroads in this point in time when the plans for your life and those for your community suddenly collide, bringing rapid change in unexpected ways. There is hidden seed lying dormant in the land of our nations. Heroes who have walked the land before us have scattered the nation with their prayers, hopes and dreams. Now it is our time for adventure. We need to agitate this seed with hope and begin to plan for our holy experiments like Penn. God spoke to me recently and said, "it is time to believe and discover what is hidden in the ground of the nations. Activate this seed – it is Kingdom seed with holy potential." We must get ready for this seed to flourish!

ACTIVATION

Which of your testimonies have overcoming power?

Write them down and stir these memories.

Ask God to strengthen you to overcome and not be overwhelmed.

Now think about the seed for this nation. What are the promises that come to your mind? What seed is in your hand for your nation?

Think about taking some time to reflect with God about this season of holy experiments.

NATIONS NEED TO BE POSSESSED

Just as we carry hope for the transformation of our regions and nations, so did Abram. God spoke to him and promised him that he would be a father to many nations and his life would be fruitful. In this season of his life, Abram had no influence and no children. This promise did not look very hopeful. But Abram did receive this promise, embraced it and let his faith and hope begin to shape his future in line with this word. Here is the word that God gave to Abram, found in Genesis:

> [4]"As for me, this is my covenant with you: You will be the father of many nations. [5]No longer will you be called Abram; your name will be Abraham, for I have made you a father of many nations. [6]I will make you very fruitful; I will make nations of you, and kings will come from you… [16]I will bless her and will surely give you a son by her. I will bless her so that she will be the mother of nations; kings of peoples will come from her."
>
> **— GENESIS 17: 4-6, 16**

As we read this scripture we should understand that we have also been given keys of destiny to birth nations and influence the leaders. This is our time to arise and birth new types of leaders and influencers in our society.

How did Abraham possess his nations and bring change? If we read this passage of scripture in Romans we can understand how this happened:

> [17]As it is written: "I have made you a father of many nations." He is our father in the sight of God, in whom he believed—the God who gives life to the dead and calls into being things that were not. [18]Against all hope, Abraham in hope believed and so became the father of many nations, just as it had been said to him, "So shall your offspring be."
>
> **— ROMANS 4:17-18**

Abraham hoped and believed, even in the face of impossibility and opposition, and so became a father of nations! I love that little phrase "…and so he became the father of many nations". Often we just want that magical "Cinderella" moment. We imagine we will hear the word, and everything will change instantaneously, of its own accord, as if by magic. But the reality is different - there is a process. Abram had to learn how to become this father in the nations! How did he do this? Abram found a new way of believing. He trained himself to see beyond what he could see naturally and see the spiritual potential and promise of God. Abram learnt how to release life into the dead and barren places and then call forth those things that did not previously exist into reality. Abram gripped and possessed his nation by faith. First he took hold of it spiritually, then he birthed its existence practically. He was a man of faith with determined hope. We also need to have this type of vital connection with our nations. We need to find our place and be the mothers and fathers in our communities. Be inspired by your vision of hope and then be the implementor of what God asks you to do. Let us arise and make a difference!

HOPE FOR THE NATIONS

When I returned to Britain, after being a missionary in Africa for eight years, I had to ask God to give me a gift of hope for this nation. When I gazed at people's faces as I walked through the town centres, or watched the mothers at the school gate, I could sense their hopelessness. People rarely smiled at you when you greeted them, voices often sounded angry or stressed, and children often cried rather than laughed. I felt the pain in the land of Britain. I began to pray and ask God to give me a word for this nation. One day, while reading Isaiah, this passage just jumped out at me. I knew this was my promise for Britain:

> [1]Arise, shine, for your light has come, and the glory of the LORD rises upon you. [2]See, darkness covers the earth and thick darkness is over the peoples, but the LORD rises upon you and his glory

appears over you. ³Nations will come to your light, and kings to the brightness of your dawn.

— ISAIAH 60:1-3

I felt God ask me if I would shine for Jesus and be a light in the dark places of this nation. God wants us to be a people of contrast, those people who bring hope into the hopeless place, light into the darkness, and His presence into the void and empty spaces. But we need to shake off the lethargy and slumber that keep us inactive and arise and shine. We have a job to do!

In these last years I have noticed many amazing people who have become part of an army of kindness that makes a difference to the lives of many. They bring hope and tangible love to the broken and overwhelmed. They are the beacons of hope in the midst of the storms of life. As we have seen earlier in this book, it takes little choices and decisions to personally walk away from the valley of troubles and through the door of hope. It is the same process for a nation too. Whether on the micro or the macro scale, there is a door of hope standing waiting for us and we need to walk through this door of life. We should ask God to touch our nation once again and enable us to see this journey of change. As the Bible says:

Ask of me, and I will make the nations your heritage, and the ends of the earth your possession.

— PSALM 2:8 (ESV)

Let us pray and ask God for revival in our nations. Church history shows us that so often, during a time when we least expect it, we see a nation turn to God. A nation can be in turmoil and hardship, yet in the middle of the chaos, people begin to find Jesus. We may look at many situations in the global scene today and only see pain and devastation but God is ready to move. Let us ask for the nations and be ready to shine with Jesus.

LIGHT IN THE DARKNESS

I have had the privilege to work with many outstanding people, both in Moldova and the Ukraine over these last years. When the war between Russia and Ukraine started in February 2022, life looked bleak. Gordon and I had been due to be in Ukraine for a Pastors' conference in March 2022 and we hoped we would still be able to go. Soon we realised that this war was not going to be a quick show of power, but a real fight for the land inch by inch. I immediately asked God how we could bring hope into this situation. Like many around the world, we raised money, sent people and food, and helped to re-house so many families displaced by this war. It often seemed as though we were just offering practical help but then we began to hear the stories:

A friend, P, told us how many pastors were enrolling in the army as chaplains, ready to help the wounded and pray with the trau-matised. P. had been asked to meet with these newly appointed army chaplains and train them to take hope to the front lines. He prayed for them to be filled with the Holy Spirit, explaining that they needed to carry hope before they could give it away. Many of the men received Jesus and were filled with the Holy Spirit. Whenever you speak to people working on the ground in the Ukraine, they tell you of the miracles happening there. People are being saved, healed and experiencing miracles as they fight to survive. One friend, J, told us of a bus with many families fleeing from Mariupol along a road to a checkpoint, when a missile began to follow this convoy on a perfect trajectory for impact. When someone in the bus cried out in prayer this bomb literally dropped out of the sky, hit the road in another area and the bus was saved.

Another woman living in the basement of a bombed apartment decided she would cook food for as many people as she could each lunchtime and evening. There were hundreds of people locked into the city, unable to leave and without food, water or heating. Our friend was taking aid into this city regularly, but the roads had been bombed and the access routes had become limited and dangerous. He had managed to keep the supplies moving for many days but now it became impossible. However, this lady had decided she would cook as usual, whether new supplies arrived or not. Each day she would go and forage in the surrounding gardens, finding vegetables left behind. She would then take her last 500g bag of pasta, remove one handful of pasta and put it back into the bag, and cook the rest. She only had this same bag and the vegetables she foraged each day for days. She chose her largest pan and cooked, never knowing how many would come for food, or how many this pan could realistically feed. Each meal fed about 150 people, and once it was 300! Every meal time she would go and get this bag of pasta and cook again, keeping one handful back. This bag lasted for eleven days, feeding hundreds, morning and night. Finally, when the food convoy got through, the supplies were able to be replenished and the 500g bag of pasta ceased to multiply!

There are so many miracle stories I could share. There was a man whose leg was shot off who was haemorrhaging severely and about to die. When the men around him prayed, the blood flow stopped and his leg was instantly healed. Stories of bullets that seemed to evaporate into thin air, food that multiplied, angels who guided people through woods and personal guides who appeared and walked children through the land-mined areas to safety. I know there have also been stories of loss and atrocities mixed with these miracles. It has been a time of miracles and great mess. But there is a spiritual hunger in the land. Pastors are reporting many people turning to Jesus and asking to be baptised. In the midst of the darkness, a light has shone.

I pray that, as you read this chapter, God is awakening in you a fresh desire to see Him move in the nations. God is not dead and the nations will see His glory. There are so many scriptures that tell us to expect life to become difficult but to also keep watching for the time of deliverance, our day of hope. So, remember, keep your confidence – God has a plan. Let us read this scripture from Hebrews:

> 35So do not throw away this confident trust in the Lord. Remember the great reward it brings you! 36Patient endurance is what you need now, so that you will continue to do God's will. Then you will receive all that he has promised. 37"For in just a little while, the Coming One will come and not delay. 38And my righteous ones will live by faith. But I will take no pleasure in anyone who turns away." 39But we are not like those who turn away from God to their own destruction. We are the faithful ones, whose souls will be saved.
>
> **— HEBREWS 10:35-39 (NLT)**

ACTIVATION

There is hope for the nations. Ask me for nations.

Ask God to show you which nations you should pray for specifically.

It is time to arise and shine in the dark places. Is there anything practical you need to do to express this light in a dark place for Jesus? Pray and listen.

Finally, ask God to remind you of miracle stories of hope in the nations and thank him for miracles in the mess.

9

With great expectations

"Fear can hold you prisoner. Hope can set you free."
— **SHAWSHANK REDEMPTION**

"If you lose hope, somehow you lose the vitality that keeps life moving, you lose that courage to be, that quality that helps you go on in spite of it all. And so today I still have a dream."
— **MARTIN LUTHER KING, JR.**

THINKING BIG

I opened my WhatsApp message to see a wonderful picture of a bride on her wedding day. She was shining with joy. Her mum was so excited and had sent me this photo and a message, thanking us for all our prayer that had led to this day. But as I looked at this happy picture further, something else also caught my attention: it was the writing on the wall behind this laughing couple. The caption read – "Think Big or you will limit me!" What a fantastic statement to encapsulate the joy and expectation of this special wedding day. Live a hope filled life with great expectation!

There are certain moments in life that just explode with hope and expectation: the day your child is born and you hold that swaddled baby and dream of all the adventures and fun you will have together; your wedding day, when you gaze into the face of your spouse and imagine your life filled with love, purpose and intimacy; the day you pick up the keys to your first home and a place where all your plans and projects to build a home will begin to unfurl; your graduation day at university; your first day at a job you have dreamed of; the moment you find Jesus and His love; discovering a great church and community of friends; and so the list could continue. These moments of exciting new opportunities stir in us a sense of great expectation. But as I considered the statement behind this bride, I realised that we have to think right in these times too. Never is there a more crucial time to have your head and heart aligned, thinking and dreaming in the same way, than when you are about to step out into a new adventure.

Too often these heights of great expectation are quickly extinguished by our rational, negative thinking that deletes these plans of hope. Our mind must be released to think big, think as God is thinking, and not as the statistics predict!

KEEP YOUR HEAD IN THE CLOUDS

As a science major, I was always taught to think in a rational, fact based way. If you cannot prove it, then you should not believe it. Find the evidence, research the statistics and believe the facts. My professional training as a research scientist was very risk averse. So when God asked me to keep my head in the clouds and dream with Him, think like Him rather than through such a narrow filter of criteria, it went against my every instinct. This conversation happened one morning when I was praying about an impossible situation and God challenged my way of thinking concerning this issue. "Rachel",

God said, "it is time to have your head in the clouds! I want you to learn to think from heaven to earth and not limit me by your earthly processing." Immediately God reminded me of this scripture that you find in the book of Colossians:

> Set your minds on things that are above, not on things that are on earth.
> — **COLOSSIANS 3:2 (ESV)**

As I contemplated this adjustment, trying to understand how to think with great expectation, God reminded me of the clouds. "Keep your head in the clouds", God had said. Often this is considered a risky affair for the dangerously dreamy. But as I considered this phrase again, God reminded me of the times I had flown into London after a ministry trip. When my head was high up in the clouds the skies were often blue, clear and sunny but, as you begin your descent, the clouds thicken, the fog descends and the rain falls. What you thought was a wonderful sunny day at 10,000 feet above London now turns out to be wet and miserable!

God was asking me to reset my reality and think from a heavenly perspective, not from the place of my earthly limitations. God wants us to put our head in the clouds and see the bigger picture through His eyes. He is asking us to think bigger, wider, differently in these days or we will limit the vision we can see. God can see the hope filled blue skies of opportunity but what we tend to see are the rain filled dismal days.

CHANGE THE DEFAULT SETTING

Usually our default setting is to be cautious. We have a tendency to be negative before we are positive; we see the weaknesses in ourselves before we can acknowledge our strengths; we feel inadequate for the task rather than qualified; we will plan smaller rather than stretch big; we will expect a minimal response rather than maximum engagement; and we like to play it safe rather than risk too much! If your mind is set on this natural default setting, thinking from this earthly perspective, you should expect to end up in the wrong place! This hope filled life is God inspired, God sustained and has to be lived in God's way. We need to reset every cautious and resistant area of our thinking to think like God. We need to be people of great expectation, ready to inspire hope in others, and lead the way.

Can you see God's big picture around you or are you limited by your inability to dream? Are you able to see more than the immediate crisis and look beyond to the door of hope? We need to see the bigger story in our journey of life.

As I was asking God to help me reset this faulty way of thinking, He challenged my ability to love myself and others. We are all familiar with God's instruction to love Him with our whole being. We read this scripture in the book of Matthew:

> [37] Jesus replied, "'You must love the LORD your God with all your heart, all your soul, and all your mind.' [38] This is the first and greatest commandment."
> — **MATTHEW 22:37-38**

We often concentrate on how we love God with our heart and soul but have you ever considered how you love God with your mind? When our heart aligns with God's heart, our passions collide, but we also need to adjust and learn to think like God too. As our love for God grows, our trust deepens and our ways of thinking expand. We begin to become risk takers and adventurers with God. Think big, remove every limitation and trust God. Now we are ready to live a hope filled life, full of expectation.

EXPECTATIONS
THAT WILL NEVER DIE

As we have explored this hope filled life, we have understood the promise of the door of hope in times of trouble, learnt to smell the scent of hope when betrayal and loss have re-shaped our tree of life and, more than anything, we now know that this hope comes from God who can fill us with fresh hope when our spiritual tanks are empty.

I pray that your life will be a life where faith, hope and love are consistently found, as Paul emphasises in his letter to the Corinthian church:

> And now these three remain: faith, hope and love. But the greatest of these is love.
> **— 1 CORINTHIANS 13:13**

What hope needs to awaken? What dreams have been downsized? Will you let hope remain and stand again beside your faith and love? Embrace hope and live a transformed life of expectation! Never forget our greatest hope of all: Jesus is coming again soon! We can read the end of the book of life, the Bible, and know that the Lamb wins, every word of promise is fulfilled, and Jesus returns to give us the gift of an eternal, hope filled life.

THERE IS HOPE

"There is hope!" - from Heaven that cry resounds;
Silencing fear, alarm - all other sounds.
"Hope!"- anchoring our souls, firm and secure;
Unwavering, unashamed, holy and pure.

"Hope and a future" - that's what God has planned.
Injecting faith and courage, so that we can stand.
Overwhelmed in our hearts by our Father's love;
Knowing He's right here, not remote or far above.

Shouts of disappointment, pain, fear and loss,
Are silenced now by the power of the Cross.
"I took it all, no need for you to fear!"
"Just trust me now! Your breakthrough is so near!"

As you pray faithfully, Father will unveil,
All of His Kingdom plans - He will never fail!
"Be joyful in hope, patient in affliction";
Live this hope filled life that once you'd thought was fiction!

Think big! No limits! Believe God has a plan!
No impossibility- shout: "I know a God who can!"
He can and will, despite all time delays.
Hold on, dig deep, and trust His perfect ways.

— Gordon Hickson
August 2023

ABOUT THE AUTHOR
RACHEL HICKSON

Rachel loves Labrador dogs, relaxing with a jigsaw puzzle, eating a good curry and sunshine! She has been married to Gordon for over 40 years. She is the mother of two married children, Nicola and David, and has six grandchildren, Leila, Cooper, Elani, Annabelle, Jeremy and Margot. Rachel loves her home, family and cooking - especially for special celebrations.

Rachel is also known as an internationally respected leader and Bible teacher with a recognised prophetic gift. She teaches all over the world and is in demand as a conference speaker. She serves several national church leadership networks where she is asked for her prophetic wisdom, insight and leadership strategy. Among other areas, Rachel is often asked to advise and support teams prophetically during times of leadership transition or major building projects and she has had the privilege of sharing in many adventures of faith in the Kingdom.

At the age of 24 Rachel, with her husband, Gordon, worked alongside Reinhard Bonnke and the Christ for all Nations team in Africa. After just six weeks in Zimbabwe, she almost lost her life in a horrific car accident, but was miraculously healed after prayer. This incident birthed in Rachel a desire to pray and to train others to realise the full potential of a praying church.

After returning from Africa in 1990, Rachel and her husband, Gordon, pastored a group of four churches in Hertfordshire, UK. It was during this time that Heartcry for Change was founded with the vision to be: "A prophetic voice with a compassionate heart".

In 2005 Rachel and Gordon moved to Oxford where Gordon was the associate minister of St. Aldates Church for 6 years. Rachel continues to travel internationally, visiting Europe, North America, Africa, SE Asia and Australia. Invitations come from a variety of denominational backgrounds, and she loves to speak to both rural and urban contexts. Rachel and Gordon still live in Oxford, UK, and love this reformation city. Together they have a passion to influence and train the next generation to be history makers.

ABOUT HEARTCRY FOR CHANGE

We work with churches and people from many nations and denominations to equip them in the following areas:

» **PRAYER** – Training an army of ordinary people in prayer schools and seminars to become confident to break the sound barrier and pray informed, intelligent and passionate prayers.

» **PROPHETIC** – Equipping the Church to be an accurate prophetic voice in the nation by teaching in training schools and conferences the principles of the prophetic gift. We seek to train people who are passionate to know the presence of God, are available to hear His voice, and then learn to speak His word with accuracy so that lives can be touched and changed.

» **WOMEN** – Delivering a message of hope to women across the nations and cultures to help them arise with a new confidence so that they can be equipped and ready to fulfil their destiny and execute their kingdom purpose.

» **CAPITAL CITIES** – Standing in the capital cities of the world, working with government institutions, businesses and the Church and then crying out for a new alignment of the natural and spiritual government in these places. A cry for London and beyond.

» **BUSINESS & FINANCE** – Connecting business people with their kingdom purpose so that provision can partner more effectively with vision and accelerate the purpose of God in nations. Connecting commerce, community and church for change!

» **LEADERS OF TOMORROW** – Mentoring and encouraging younger leaders to pioneer the next move of God in the areas of politics and government, social action and justice issues, creative arts, media and the ministry.

» **NATIONS** - Partnering with nations, like Moldova, by supplying teaching, training and practical resources to strengthen and resource them as they work for breakthrough in their nations.

» **SOCIAL MEDIA** – To be a regular voice of hope and encouragement through social media, via YouTube and Facebook. Providing regular teaching on relevant topics to help people keep their perspective in their everyday life.

» **RESOURCES & CONFERENCES** – Writing books, manuals and training materials that will equip the church prophetically. Hosting Legacy Days where leaders and church members can be refreshed and refocussed in the presence of God.

HEARTCRY FOR CHANGE UK
CMS House,
Watlington Rd,
OXFORD,
OX4 6BZ
www.heartcry.co.uk
www.heartcryforchange.com

HEARTCRY FOR CHANGE USA
c/o Rainier Hills Christian Fellowship
23711 Entwhistle Rd E
Buckley
WA 98321
www.heartcry.us

FOLLOW RACHEL AND THE TEAM ON FACEBOOK
www.facebook.com/Heartcryforchange

OTHER BOOKS WRITTEN BY RACHEL HICKSON

SHE IS THE AUTHOR OF 12 BOOKS:

» Supernatural Communication, the Privilege of Prayer,
» Supernatural Breakthrough, The Heartcry for Change,
— PUBLISHED BY NEW WINE MINISTRIES.

» Stepping Stones to Freedom,
» Pathway of Peace,
» Run your Race.
» Eat the Word, Speak the Word
— PUBLISHED BY MONARCH

» Eat the Word Study Guide,
» Supernatural Communication Study Guide,
» Release My Frozen Assets
» Eat the Word, Speak the Word - 2nd Edition
» I Love Prayer
» Spiritual Architects
— PUBLISHED BY HEARTCRY FOR CHANGE.

GORDON HAS WRITTEN ONE BOOK:
» Harnessed for Adventure, A personal story of our lives
— PUBLISHED BY HEARTCRY FOR CHANGE

HOW TO ORDER OTHER BOOKS

Heartcry for Change published titles can be purchased through our website: www.heartcryforchange. com/shop in paperback and e-book formats.

Harnessed for Adventure is also available as an audiobook. Payment can be made in GBP £ or USD $ using a debit or credit card or PayPal.

All of the books are also available on Amazon.

Printed in Great Britain
by Amazon

40320093R00089